P9-DCH-258

Britannica Bookshelf-Great Lives

Making Music
LEONARD BERNSTEIN

Britannica Bookshelf-Great Lives

Making Music

LEONARD BERNSTEIN

by Shirley Bernstein

Published by
ENCYCLOPAEDIA BRITANNICA PRESS, INC., *Chicago*

TABLE OF CONTENTS

LIST OF ILLUSTRATIONS

To Jamie, Alexander, and Nina

Chapter 1

Lenny

To millions of television-watching Americans, Leonard Bernstein is a teacher of the musical arts. To the theater-going public he is a composer in the musical theater. To the concert-going public he is a composer-pianist and the conductor of the New York Philharmonic, one of the world's great orchestras. To me he is Lenny—my brother.

My earliest memory of Lenny is not a musical one. I remember him first as a ten-year-old boy with test tube and pipet, hard at work up in the attic of our house in Boston, Massachusetts. He was trying to distill pure alcohol from rubbing alcohol. Lenny and his best friend Eddie Ryack went at it with the earnestness and dedication of boy-Pasteurs on the brink of a great discovery.

Though contemptuous of my baby years, they yielded to my mother's plea, "Let Shirley play with you," and tolerantly dubbed me their mascot, which made my unwanted presence in their laboratory a little more acceptable to everyone. My main job there was to sit still and keep quiet.

These excursions into the world of science came to nothing, but such matters seemed to have held a powerful fascination for young Lenny. He has told me that his own first memory involves a very special scientific experiment. When he was about four years old, he heard that man was made of dust. Taking this piece of information literally, he proceeded to test the theory. He collected some whorls of dust from under a bed, put them in the bathroom sink, and turned on the water. His goal—to make a human being! The experiment ended disastrously, not only in keen disappointment for Lenny at seeing his potential man become a puddle of watery mud, but also in considerable financial loss for my parents. Lenny had managed to turn the faucet on, but in his panic he couldn't manage to turn it off. Frightened, he stole out of the bathroom, hoping the faucet would somehow magically turn itself off. An hour later, my mother walked into a bathroom ankle-deep in water. What was worse, the water had gone through the ceiling of the apartment below ours, where a tailor and his family lived. Many suits and dresses the tailor had brought home to be worked on were completely ruined by the aftermath of Lenny's people-making test. The bill for the sodden clothes was paid by my dismayed parents.

Although chemistry eventually lost its attraction for Lenny, the force behind that attraction never left him, a force that is, I think, a vital element in the development of any talent—curiosity. This wondering about why things are, and how, and what if, and then finding out by asking, by reading, or by doing—this kind of curiosity belongs not only to the bright child. If you're lucky you have it all your life. Lenny has it. There's always something new for him to find out about, or something already known for him to rediscover, new values for him to hunt out, a fresh approach for him to experiment with.

Young Lenny and Shirley

Bernstein Collection

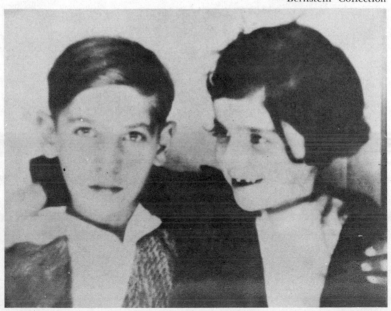

This quality keeps Lenny ardently young. It makes every project he tackles an adventure, and most especially it feeds his innate love and understanding for children. Sometimes he has tried to express that understanding in his music. When he was 21 years old, he wrote a group of songs called *I Hate Music,* five children's songs to be sung by a grown-up soprano as if she were a ten-year-old girl. One of these songs tells how the girl feels when her curiosity makes grown-ups laugh at her and not understand. One song goes like this:

> *"I just found out today*
> *That I'm a person too,*
> *Like you.*
> *. . . I have lots of thoughts;*
> *Like what's behind the sky;*
> *And what's behind what's*
> *   behind the sky:*
> *But ev'ryone says, 'Isn't*
> *   she sweet? She wants to*
> *   know everything!'*
>
> *Don't you? . . .*
> *I'm a person too, like you!"*

I remember Lenny from the time he found out that he "was a person too." In this book I'm going to try to tell you something about that early time and about the boy who grew up to be, among other things, America's

Shirley, Sam, Jennie, and Lenny

first homegrown, home-taught conductor of a major symphony orchestra. It began this way.

Until he was ten years old, Lenny's childhood was unusual only in that he was sick more than most children. He had what was referred to in the family as "a delicate chest," a condition that accounted for frequent and lengthy bouts with colds, bronchitis, and asthma. It would give a nice, dramatic touch to be able to say that this little boy, sick in bed, lay listening to his first symphonies, dreaming of composing and conducting his own when he grew up. But I can't say it because nothing like that happened. Lenny didn't know what a symphony was then, nor had he ever heard one.

Our father and mother were—and still are—good and loving parents, intent on giving their children everything they could think of to help them grow up

[*17*]

healthy and happy. We lived in pleasant houses; our mother concentrated on getting nourishing food into our stomachs; our father began planning and saving for our college educations. That there was an absence of music in the house was not uncommon, especially in those days when radios were owned only by the few. We had one, but if there was serious music on it, we didn't know it. Television was still 25 years away. To hear music, you had to go to a concert hall or play it yourself. Nobody we knew went to concerts, and we had no piano.

And then suddenly we had a piano—and that's how Lenny's musical life began. The arrival of the piano was sheer accident. An aunt who was moving away to another city needed a place to store her ungainly upright piano, and our living room became that storage place.

Love of music came instantly and strongly for Lenny. Once that piano had come, been seen, and had utterly conquered him, there was never afterward any question in his mind but that music was what he wanted. He asked immediately and heatedly for lessons.

He began with piano lessons from a neighborhood teacher, Freda Carp, who came to the house once a week. Just as did thousands of other boys and girls throughout the country, he struggled through John Williams' *First Grade Piano Book*. What was different was Lenny's feeling about the piano, his excitement as he began to see what beauty of sound he might one day be able to make. He would sit for hours, his preparations for the following week's lesson long done, noodling, improvising, searching out the mysteries the instrument held for him. He never had to be reminded to practice; the trick was to get him away from the piano, to rest my parents' ears, and to let his little sister sleep.

The coming of music into his life worked some sort of magic for Lenny. He had found an excitement that has never left him, and a world of his own that he can never leave. Whether or not it was a direct result, there was immediately a marked improvement in his physical condition. His ailments began to leave him, he grew taller and stronger, and he became an exuberant leader among his friends instead of the wistful, skinny little boy he had been, peering in from the fringe of the group.

He attended Boston Public Latin School, academically the most difficult school in Boston, and he did well. The school required its students to take six years of Latin, as well as two other languages. Lenny chose French and German. Along with the ancient Latin language, he began to learn an even older language. Every day after his regular school, he went for an hour and a half to Hebrew school, where he was taught the Bible, the history of the Jews, and Hebrew. That was a lot of schooling, but Lenny thrived on it—he loved to learn. In case that sounds as if he were too good to be true, a teachers pet kind of boy—he wasn't. He was full of mischief, with more than his share of the unruly behaviour common to little boys.

Because my father was a deeply religious man, his children were often taken to services at the Temple, as we called the synagogue. Curiously, Lenny's first real experience with some of the great composers of the past was in the Temple. The one we attended was a beautiful, big white building; and, more to the point, it had a gifted cantor, a first-rate choir, and Solomon Braslavsky. He was the organist and choirmaster, a man who adored music and was well trained in it. He made of his duties in the Temple something more than the simple supplying of music suitable for religious service. Using the talents of the sweet-voiced cantor and his disciplined choir to the fullest, Professor Brasslovsky would make impressive arrangements of the litanies and hymns, arrangements highly influenced by many of the great composers of the past. Lenny and I can still sing much of what we heard there in those early years. Now we recognize the sounds of Giuseppe Verdi, Ernest Bloch, Modest Mussorgsky, Felix Mendelssohn, and Franz Schubert. When we first heard them, we thought it was all Professor Braslavsky.

The music heard in the Temple helped to make the time spent there a moving experience for Lenny. His composing career reflects the influence of that experience. His first big work was the *Jeremiah Symphony;* he has written a setting of the prayer Hashkivenu, part of the Sabbath service; and he has just recently finished a *Choral Symphony* based on the traditional Kaddish or Prayer For the Dead.

Until he was about 15 years old, Lenny behaved toward me pretty much as all older brothers behave toward their younger sisters. He liked me all right, but we didn't have too much in common. He was greatly given to pushing me around. The house rang daily with cries of "Mamma, Lenny hit me." And then one day, we began to be good friends—through music.

At the age of nine, I too had begun to take piano lessons. My teacher pronounced me talented, but that wasn't enough to make me practice. It was very hard for me to practice my scales and my simple little pieces when I heard Lenny pounding away at the Grieg *Concerto* and other hard pieces. He didn't play them well yet, but he made a brave try at it. The difference between my faltering little sounds and what seemed to me his big sure ones was enough to discourage me. So my lessons stopped. But my interest in and love for music went on, and bloomed under Lenny's informal teaching.

He had just heard about opera. His curiosity led him to the public library, where he took out whole opera scores. We would learn them together. Eagerness and the innocence of not knowing any better gave us the courage to plough into *Aida* with a thoroughness and zest that the more experienced might have balked at. Lenny sang all the men's parts; I sang all the women's parts. We both sang the choruses. It was a breathless business, what with Lenny's tinny tenor, my piping soprano, a complete ignorance of Italian, and Lenny's still imperfect technique at handling masses of notes —and *Aida* is full of masses of notes.

[21]

In spite of everything, however, we had a great time. From *Aida* we went on to *Carmen, La Boheme,* and *Madame Butterfly.* We would sit for hours on end—as if, my mother said, we were "chained to the piano"—screaming at the top of our lungs, filled with wonder and enormous excitement at being able to make the beautiful music "happen" by ourselves. Since neither of us had ever heard *Aida* or any other opera before, we were beautifully unaware of how it was supposed to sound; so we had no self-consciousness about it. We just sailed into it, all flags flying.

The seeds of masterly, creative teaching were already sprouting fast in Lenny. He demanded my best, but he had great patience and an amazing skill for one so young in communicating the inner meaning of the music. And above all, even then, he made it all such fun.

Audiences see Lenny now, an assured musician, all grown up, in full control of his craft. I see that, too, but sometimes when I'm at one of his concerts, I get a double image, and see superimposed on the conductor of the New York Philharmonic a 15-year-old boy, breathlessly playing and singing at the piano with a blazing innocence, a tender dedication, aware of no other world at those moments than the one of his own making.

Chapter 2

Bring on the Dancing Girls

From the summer when Lenny was 11 years old until he was 14, he went to camp. He became an expert young athlete, winning the Best All-Round Camper's Cup, and medals for diving, dramatics, and for his fast blooming ability to get on well with other children.

By the time he was 15, the family had bought a summer house in Sharon, Massachusetts, a pretty little lakeside village some twenty miles south of Boston. The first summer there, Lenny's restless energies found an outlet in putting on a production, unorthodox to say the least, of Bizet's *Carmen*.

With another boy named Dana Schnittkind, Lenny replaced the French words with lyrics in English that included local jokes, slang expressions, and boyish hijinks. Nevertheless the new libretto stayed true to the original story line of the fiery Spanish cigarette girl and her two sweethearts, the soldier Don José and the toreador Escamillo. Since none of the youngsters rounded up to play in the opera could begin to measure up to the vocal demands of the score, the coadaptors decided the only thing to do was to exploit that lack and have fun with the very weakness of the cast. So the girls sang the men's parts, and the boys sang the women's roles. Lenny, got up in a Spanish shawl and a black wig, was the heroine Carmen, and his current girl friend, Beatrice Gordon, in matador pants and a charcoal mustache, sang Don José. Co-collaborator Dana Schnittkind in a blond, pigtailed wig and a white dress, played the part of Micaela, Don José's castoff girl friend. I, shaking with fright and voice atremble, read the Prologue in my best party dress.

The following summer, about thirty of us found ourselves up to our ears in daily rehearsals for a production of Gilbert and Sullivan's *The Mikado*. Lenny learned the operetta himself, teaching it at the same time to me, cut it, assigned the roles to the most likely seeming young people available, assembled the props and made the scenery, produced the show, directed it, and played Nanki-Poo, the leading man's role. When Lenny wasn't on stage, he raced around to the wings to take over at the old upright piano, relieving the girl—named, if I remember aright, Ruth Potash—who played while he was on stage. I was given the leading lady's part of Yum-Yum. No one ever questioned this bit of casting. I already knew the part, and I suppose that all the singing I had been doing for a year learning operas with Lenny had given me a confidence no other little girl felt ready to challenge.

Rehearsals were held every afternoon for a month in our living room. My mother's patience was something to marvel at. Strewn around our living room were 30-odd young performers, draped carelessly over the furniture and sprawled on the floor, singing away at the top of their voices to Lenny's direction from the piano. Every afternoon, midway in the proceedings, the bells of the ice-cream truck would ring and there would be a dash into the street. Lenny's authority and dignity as producer-director didn't interfere with his leading the race out the door for the ice cream. Then back we would all troop, ice creams dripping, our sticky hands leaving marks all over my mother's furniture, as we settled down to another hour of rehearsal.

All this while, three-year-old Burtie, our baby brother, was having his afternoon nap! What's more, he slept through it. I think he was already so used to a musical racket while he slept that the absence of it would have awakened him. At the age of three, he had already been exposed to Lenny's teaching. Lenny had taught him to recognize and name several thematic bits of music. In response to a few bars of Wagner's *Die Walküre*, his baby treble would shout out in triumph, "That's the Ride of the Val-*kee*-ree."

[25]

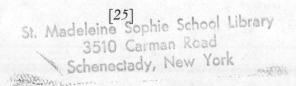

But during our *Mikado* rehearsals he slept. We called ourselves The Sharon Players, and put the show on at the local town hall. What with doting parents and tolerant neighbors, we performed to a sold-out house at $1 a ticket. After paying for the rental of the hall, the remaining proceeds were given to charity, except for 75 cents per player, which we spent at the local Howard Johnson's in whatever stomach-turning way we chose. Seventy-five cents went much further in those days than it does now. To use up our salary, led by Lenny's daring, we each consumed a hot dog, a royal banana split, a double-thick frosted, and a big bag of popcorn. There were many sick stomachs that night, but nonetheless a bunch of very happy youngsters.

The next year we put on Gilbert and Sullivan's *H.M.S. Pinafore*. Lenny was in an expansive mood that summer. He had graduated from Latin School and had just been informed that Harvard had accepted him in its freshman class. That was enough to give any boy a heady feeling. He plunged with even more than his usual exuberance into a bang-up production of *Pinafore*. This time there were a couple of switches in casting. I didn't get the lead because we had discovered from snatches of song delivered by our maid as she went about her housework that she had a perfectly marvelous voice. Lenny broke the news to me gently that he had cast her in the lead. Though my ego was bruised, I had to admit that the best voice should have the part, and there was no question but that our Italian songbird had the best voice. Lenny also demoted himself from the leading tenor role of Ralph Rackstraw. For one thing his tenor had descended to baritone; for another, a boy had turned up with a voice much closer to a real singing sound than Lenny could get near. (His name was Victor Alpert. Today he is the librarian of the Boston Symphony Orchestra.) For all of his musical talents, Lenny's voice was, and remains today, an object of affectionate family derision.

Denying himself the pretty arias and duets of the tenor role, he assigned himself the baritone part of Captain Corcoran, which was less demanding vocally. Wanting to make up to me my loss of the lead, he kindly arranged to put into *Pinafore* a special dancing sequence, starring me as an Egyptian high priestess, and my twin girl friends as my handmaidens! How could he work a high priestess into a very British operetta? Simple! He had the captain of the *Pinafore,* eager to impress the visiting admiral, Sir Joseph Porter, blithely invent an exotic entertainment for him. At a suitable place in the story, the captain called out, "Bring on the dancing girls," and out I floated, clad in yards of cheesecloth, to the accompaniment of the ballet music from *Aida!* This little number represented Lenny's first and last attempt as a choreographer, but it was a dilly.

As for our maid, she was a smash hit. Again, my mother's angelic good humour must be noted. With an unbelieving, slightly glazed look in her eyes, she would stand, dustcloth in hand, watching her maid march off

[27]

to rehearsal with her two children, leaving her to make the beds and wash the dishes. There were moments of protest from her, but Lenny was a persuasive talker; and he got his "star" sufficient time off from her household duties to be able to come to all the rehearsals.

Lenny put everything he had into those Gilbert and Sullivan productions. Amateur and sweet-silly as they were, they reflected all the qualities he was to retain and deepen as he grew up: invention, authority, humor, ease of communication, and perhaps most important of all—enthusiasm.

Wherever he goes now, and whatever he does, it's as if he takes those years with him, transferring that same enthusiasm and youthful excitement to whatever project is before him. As long as he keeps those qualities —and I think he'll have them all his life—his work will bring his listeners great pleasure and himself great joy.

Chapter 3

"Father's Sorrow, Father's Joy"

Through all time, fathers have been upset and saddened when their sons chose a profession that for one
reason or another seemed an undesirable choice to the
fathers. Our father, in his view, had one reason *and*
another.

He had emigrated all alone from Russia when he
was 16 years old, full of excitement and hope. The first
years were hard, as they were for most of the immigrants coming here in those years. Our father Samuel
supported himself cleaning fish while he went to night
school to learn the language of his new country. He
finally got a good job in the beauty-parlor supply business; and within a very few years, he was on his way
to becoming a successful business man. He married our

pretty mother, Jennie, and a year later Lenny was born. Our father put all his dreams into this little boy. He wanted his son, born in the United States, to have the best in life. He thought that material comforts and the best possible education for his son might make up for his own deprivation and lack of freedom suffered in tsarist Russia during his own childhood.

When Lenny first began to show signs of loving music, my father wasn't at all disturbed. It would be a nice hobby and relaxation for him one day. All my father had known of music in Russia was the street musicians who wandered through the villages, to whom the people threw a kopeck or two in exchange for a tune scraped on a fiddle. Such musicians were considered to be little better than beggars. Memories of them came back to haunt him when Lenny would talk excitedly about how much he loved music, and how he would one day be a real musician. It was impossibly hard for my father to imagine the achievement of real success as a serious musician, even in America.

And there was another reason for my father's hostility to Lenny's dream of being a musician. My father had worked very hard and had made his own business, the Samuel J. Bernstein Hair Company, a solid success. What father who is the head of a self-made business does *not* dream of his son's joining him in it and one day taking it over? It is, after all, a kind of immortality for a man, to have his name and work continue on in his son after he is gone.

[*30*]

At the beginning, when Lenny first started piano lessons, there was no trouble. The lessons had continued with the teachers changing as Lenny's rapidly improving technique warranted. After four years, he found his first really good teacher, Helen Coates, assistant to the finest piano teacher in Boston, Heinrich Gebhard. (Helen is still with Lenny today, having served as his extraordinarily efficient and devoted secretary since 1944.)

Lenny remained with Helen, and eventually Mr. Gebhard, for seven years, studying enormous amounts of piano repertory and learning everything they had to teach him about music in general. During these years our father, seeing how intense his son's interest in music

Lenny as graduate, age 15

Lenny at the piano, age 16

had become, began to balk. The lessons were expensive, but what disturbed our father much, much more was the dawning realization that Lenny did indeed mean to make music his life work. Now began the conflict of wills, a show of determination on both their parts.

Our father tried refusing to pay for the lessons; Lenny paid for them out of his allowance. Our father tried cutting off the allowance; Lenny worked Saturday nights in a high school jazz band to get the money for his lessons. At this point, impressed by the passion of his son's resolution, our father weakened, restored the allowance, and continued to pay for the lessons.

In spite of his objections, there had been some pleasure for our father in Lenny's music, some sort of fringe benefits. When Lenny was 15 years old, my father took him along on a holiday cruise to the West Indies. Lenny's great shipboard success, to which his piano playing contributed greatly, made my father glow with pride in his son. Another time, at a special evening program given by the brotherhood of the synagogue we all attended, Lenny played a piece of his own—well, sort of his own. He took a well-known theme sung by the choir during services, and played it in the manner of three famous composers, his conception of how the Polish Frédéric Chopin, the Hungarian Franz Liszt, and the American George Gershwin might have dealt with this material. His performance was a big hit, and my father basked in the warmth of the congratulations given him by his friends.

He recognized the talent in his son, admired it and was proud; but these feelings were not enough to soothe his fears about the boy's future. One summer he asked Lenny to try to learn his beauty-parlor supply business, to work in the shipping room at a fair salary. Lenny did try. He went to work every morning with our father for two whole weeks. Lenny did his work conscientiously and well, but he felt no satisfaction in his achievements, nor any pleasure in considering the advancements that were sure to come.

It was now abundantly and irrevocably clear, even to our father, that it was going to be music for Lenny. Lenny knew that the future would be unsure, but he also knew that music was his love, and he had to pursue it.

Sometimes you hear or read about someone who insists he could have been a fine musician or writer or painter, if only his parents hadn't made it impossible for him. I wouldn't believe such a protesting person for a minute. If the talent is truly there, no obstacles are going to keep it from being born and flourishing. If anything, I have a feeling that a little parental discouragement, in a funny way, can help. If the talent is small, or isn't really there, parental objections can dampen the youngster's conviction about himself and help guide him into a profession more truly suited to him. But if there is real talent and the strong need to express it, the discouragement will first lead to careful self-questioning; and then if the youngster still feels sure his life work must be in the arts, he will be strengthened in his decision to go after it.

That's the way it worked with Lenny. By the time he was 21, my father began to bow to the inevitable; and though he worried a great deal about Lenny's future, he began to take more and more pride in his accomplishments, the early small ones, and then within only four years, enough achievement and recognition to make any father glow with pleasure. Today there is no prouder father anywhere in the world. Though he hadn't wanted music as a profession for his son, he loved him enough to want him to be happy, to find his dream. Even as our father grumbled and protested through those early years, he respected what Lenny was trying to do and be. If our father had had his way, of course his son would not have become a musician; but nevertheless Lenny's success, unexpected though it was to our father, grew out of the fabric of his own hopes and dreams.

Lenny's first big work, the *Jeremiah Symphony*, is dedicated to our father—in love and gratitude.

Chapter *4*

College Days

Lenny had just turned 17, and it was time to begin
college. Life at Harvard was a happy time for him. There
was contact with the probing minds of its fine faculty,
association with boys of widely varied backgrounds, a
full campus life, and concentrated work in many different studies, including music with Walter Piston and
Edward Burlingame Hill. Everything contributed to his
fast growing maturity.

He enjoyed his studies at Harvard, but he was far
from being a grind, as several C's scattered through his
grades attest. He almost got into real scholastic trouble
once—in his senior year. Busy with writing his thesis
and with many extracurricular activities, he had severely neglected a political science course, one that had seen

[37]

little of Lenny in the classroom. Since he had cut so many of the lectures, he had to study the course almost from scratch the night before the final exam in a wild scramble to stuff the material into his head. To flunk a course at the end of his senior year, of course, would put his graduation in jeopardy—so the heat was on. Along with some other classmates in similar trouble, who had mysteriously obtained detailed course outlines and some caffeine pills, Lenny sat up all night cramming for the final examination.

At nine in the morning, without having gone to bed at all and with his nerves jangling from the caffeine, he went to take the exam. The major question to be answered in the two-hour period was "Compare Europe before and after 1848," a question requiring far-reaching and specific knowledge for its answer. Lenny's mind went blank, as one's mind will do when it has been pushed so hard to retain thousands of facts all at once. It's a tribute to the all-around education Lenny had received at Harvard, to his own wits, and to his ability to think on the spur of the moment that, faced with the impossibility of answering the question in any expected style, he was able to fill several bluebooks with poetry quotations, drawings, snatches of music, and other thoroughly unorthodox material. Somehow all of it turned out to be pertinent and impressive. The result was a grade of A-plus on the examination, with a comment from the professor that Lenny's was one of the most brilliant examination papers he had ever read.

By the end of his senior year, Lenny had been actively involved in several different kinds of musical events. He had become a markedly good pianist and had played with the Massachusetts State Symphony Orchestra. He had composed and conducted music for a student production of Aristophanes' comedy *The Birds*; and in the last months of his senior year he produced and co-directed for the Harvard Student Union an astonishingly good production of Marc Blitzstein's music-drama *The Cradle Will Rock,* based on the timely subject of the workers' struggle in Steeltown to form a union. This show had the year before stood the New York theater-going public on its collective ear. Now this one-night student production, sponsored by such Harvard faculty members as historian Arthur Schlesinger, Sr. and poet Archibald MacLeish, roused Eliot Norton, the top theater critic of the Boston *Post* to say in his review: "Last night's performance was given with fire, ardor and intelligence by the most talented student cast this department has ever seen." I sang the leading role of the Moll in this production. No one guessed that I was only 15 years old. The critics, the audience, and the faculty assumed I was a student from nearby Radcliffe.

The show caused such excitement that a second demand performance was given the following week. The composer-author Marc Blitzstein came to Cambridge to see and hear this performance of his work. He was surprised and delighted to find this student company giving such a professional performance. He even went so far as to say that much of the production compared favorably with that of the New York company. From this happy beginning, Marc and Lenny's friendship has remained strong and lasting for more than 20 years.

In that year of 1939, Lenny met two more musicians of established talent and reputation, composer Aaron Copland and conductor Dimitri Mitropoulos. Both these men were to have considerable influence on Lenny's later decision to study conducting.

The specifics of how, when, where, and what kind of musical work Lenny was going to do were murky and elusive to him. Conducting was as yet an unborn thought. Up to this time, he had more or less taken it for granted that he would be a pianist. But a future as a concert pianist didn't seem to Lenny to be as fulfilling a prospect as he had once thought it would be. Why? Twenty years later it could be said that although he didn't know it then, a big talent for conducting was lying dormant in him, quietly waiting for him to discover and use it, not yet announcing itself but creating a vaguely reasoned though strongly felt dissatisfaction with the idea of becoming a concert pianist. Maybe it's true, or maybe playing the piano did not fully satisfy his need for one hundred percent involvement in his work; or maybe he thought he wasn't really good enough to become a top-ranking pianist. He has told me that he couldn't face the prospect of endless touring, playing the same Beethoven sonatas and Chopin etudes over and over again night after night in one city after another.

Aaron Copland and Lenny, 1962

[*41*]

Any or all of these theories may be true—even Lenny himself isn't sure today what really stirred him to study conducting. There's no question, though, that he was strongly affected by meeting Copland and Mitropoulos, both of whom suggested that he become a conductor. Both felt that Lenny's extraordinary sense of music, his already highly developed comprehensive knowledge of it, his enthusiasm for all kinds of good music, and the articulate and meaningful way he could communicate that enthusiasm—all these things gave him the stuff of which good conductors are made.

It wasn't an easy decision for Lenny to make. First of all, there was our father, viewing with sharp disapproval plans for further musical study. It was a matter of "Millions for education but not one more cent for music." So right after graduating from Harvard, Lenny went to New York. The years of formal education were over. Now he had to get his postgraduate bearings. What was he going to do or be now that the sheltering years of school were over?

Lenny moved into an uncomfortable but cheap apartment in Greenwich Village, sharing it with a good friend, Adolph Green. He had first met Adolph two years before at, of all places, Camp Onota in western Massachusetts. "Uncle Lenny," as musical counselor, had put the campers to work learning Gilbert and Sullivan's *Pirates of Penzance*. But there was no one around big enough or old enough to play the principal part

of the Pirate King. The camp's drama counselor reported to Lenny that he had a friend in New York
who loved and knew incredible amounts of all kinds of
music. He had been spending the hot summer working
as a runner on Wall Street, and probably wouldn't be
averse to coming to the cool Berkshires for a couple of
weeks. Lenny said, "Fine. Get him."

Adolph came, was a great Pirate King, and became
one of Lenny's best friends. More than 25 years of
friendship has seen them come from the "What-am-I-
going-to-be-when-I-grow-up?" years, through periods of
discouragement, and into the time of great success for
both, each having reached the top of his respective
profession. Adolph is half of the team of Betty Comden
and Adolph Green, who have achieved great success as
writers for motion pictures and the theater, and as
lyricists and performers. They have done two Broadway
shows with Lenny, *On the Town* and *Wonderful Town*,
about which we will hear more later, and many
others. Lenny is godfather to Adolph's son as Adolph is
to Lenny's.

But during that summer in 1939 when they shared
an apartment in the Village, neither boy had the
faintest idea of what to do, how to begin his adult life.
The summer months went by. Lenny had tried to find a
job without success. Finally, without funds or ideas, he
had to go back home to Boston.

He had been home only a few days when he heard
that Fritz Reiner was still able to accept a scholarship

[*43*]

student in his small conducting class at the Curtis Institute of Music in Philadelphia. At the last minute, Lenny got an appointment for an audition with Reiner; rushed off to Philadelphia to see him; and, to his astonishment and joy, was accepted by the maestro, as a distinguished conductor is called.

Lenny came back to Boston to announce his acceptance. His excitement was quieted by the realization that there was going to be trouble with our father.

Lenny's going to Curtis seemed to our father a thoroughly fruitless venture. You have to remember that this was in 1939; and at that time there was not one major—or creditable minor—orchestra in the country led by a conductor who had been born and trained in America. To give an idea of how completely closed the doors were, this is how the lineup looked:

The New York Philharmonic, John Barbirolli, born in England, then nearly 40 years old.

The Boston Symphony, Serge Koussevitsky, born in Russia, then 65 years old.

The Philadelphia Orchestra, Eugene Ormandy, born in Hungary, then nearly 40 years old.

The San Francisco Symphony, Pierre Monteux, born in France, and then 64 years old.

The Minneapolis Orchestra, Dimitri Mitropoulos, born in Greece, then 43 years old.

The Chicago Symphony, Frederick Stock, born in Germany, then nearly 67 years old.

The NBC Symphony, Arturo Toscani, born in Italy, then 72 years old.

Ormandy was considered the "baby" of the group, and he was nearly 40 years old. (Barbirolli's U. S. conductorship lasted only five years.) So there was good reason for a father to shake his head pessimistically at the idea that a boy in his early 20's, even one thoroughly trained and qualified, would have a chance.

But Lenny was not about to be dissuaded. He borrowed some money for his expenses in the first semester, packed his bags, kissed us all goodbye, crossed his fingers, and was off to Philadelphia.

Life at Curtis was lonely. He was the only student who was a college graduate, and therefore his fellow students distrusted him. Most of them had arrived at Curtis as little piano or violin geniuses when they were about eight years old. They were cool to Lenny, the newcomer. As a result, his best friend was a teacher, with whom he has remained on close and affectionate terms. Lenny had little money and relatively few friends; but the work, though hard and demanding, made up for a lot. He was becoming a really fine pianist now under the disciplined and brilliant teaching of Madame Isabelle Vengerova.

Lenny was terrified of Madame Vengerova at first. A brilliant teacher and a sharp disciplinarian, she made Lenny walk a very fine line, demanding nothing less than his deepest concentration, his best effort every

[45]

time he touched the key of the piano. His fear of her eventually subsided, though he continued to call her effectionately "Tirana"—the feminine form of the Russian word for tyrant. Until her death in 1956, Lenny remained her admiring friend and sometime pupil.

Once when Lenny was conducting the Philharmonic, Madame Vengerova came to a rehearsal to listen to him conduct a Mozart concerto from the piano. When she saw Lenny after the rehearsal, Vengerova, uncowed by her former pupil's fame and achievements, upbraided him for what she considered some ill considered moments in his performance. She said sternly, "If your orchestra played like that, you would leave the stage." There followed a lengthy work session on the concerto. After the performance the night of the concert, Madame Vengerova came backstage and beamed. Her student had done well.

At Curtis, Lenny was learning the craft and developing the art of composing under the composer Randall Thompson. And he was taking his first baby steps in conducting. Fritz Reiner, his teacher in conducting, was everything Lenny had hoped he would be. He was a taskmaster, demanding of his student that he pursue perfection of technique and complete knowledge of the matter at hand. Reiner drilled into Lenny a principle that he often cites as the first rule of being a conductor: *Don't go near the podium unless you know every note of the piece you're going to conduct.* Every beginner in a profession should be taught to work thus.

Fritz Reiner

In those years, as I've pointed out, the chances for a young American to become the conductor of an orchestra were so slight as to be almost nonexistent. The opportunities even to study conducting, especially with a renowned maestro, were almost as hard to come by. Lenny was lucky.

During the winter of 1939-1940, Lenny studied with Reiner, and in the following summer Lenny was accepted at the Berkshire Music Center, which had just opened. There his teacher was Serge Koussevitsky. Reiner and Koussevitsky! Reiner and Koussevitsky were utterly different from each other as teachers and conductors, and both of them were masters.

In temperament, Koussevitsky was exactly the opposite of Reiner. With Reiner, thoroughness in knowledge of technique and the composer's intent came first. With Koussevitsky it was the handling of the emotional response to music that took first place. One man went first to the mind, the other to the heart of music. To

[47]

have the teaching of both of these great musicians, one offsetting and complementing the other, for two winters and two summers during the same formative period gave Lenny a completeness of training and a depth of inspiration that few students are privileged to have.

Chapter 5

Sergei Alexandrovitch

Lenny's deep friendship with Koussevitsky was to become one of the most important in his life. But that first summer he was just one of five boys, all students in the first class of a new and exciting venture. Lenny's fellow students were Lukas Foss, now a famous composer and professor at the University of California at Los Angeles in charge of symphony and advanced composition; Thor Johnson, now director of musical activities at Northwestern University in Evanston, Illinois, and a noted conductor; Walter Hendl, associate conductor of the Chicago Symphony Orchestra with Fritz Reiner and musical director of the Ravinia (Illinois) Festival; and Richard Korn, conductor of the Orchestra of America.

Serge Koussevitsky

Serge Koussevitsky was then 66 years old and had been the conductor of the Boston Symphony Orchestra for more than 17 years. He was a man of magnetic personality, handsome, warmly charming, highly emotional—and one of the great conductors of the world by the agreement of music critics and musicians. What might be considered alienating flaws in another man became in Koussevitsky part of his special charm and noble conceit. Once, after a concert at Tanglewood, a breathless lady came backstage to see him, filled with the beauty of the Brahms symphony she had just heard. She blurted out, "Oh, Dr. Koussevitsky—you are—you're—God!" To which extravagant compliment, Koussevitsky replied by shrugging eloquently and saying, "Ah yes, Madame, but think of the responsibility."

Koussevitsky conceived of nothing, including himself, on a small scale. In accordance, his most cherished dream was a big one. He wanted to found a school to which the most talented young musicians in the country might come, on scholarship if they couldn't afford it, and not only study with the best obtainable faculty of practicing musicians, but also begin to use their talents for the public and critics to view. In other words, he was trying to fill a gaping hole in the scheme of American musical life, a place where the highly trained but not yet-professional young musician could begin to lose his amateur status. Unlike Europe, with its resident orchestra and opera house in almost every city of any size where young musicians could begin their professional lives, America had only five or six good orchestras and three opera houses. And the opportunities in these few places were almost completely filled by transplanted Europeans. There was no place for the American musician to begin his apprenticeship. Koussy wanted to provide that place. And the Berkshire Music Center was it.

Tanglewood, as it is better known, is situated on a beautiful estate of that name in Lenox and Stockbridge, Massachusetts. The entire Boston Symphony is in residence there during the summer and gives a series of concerts over a six-week period. That's the festival part of Tanglewood. It attracts many thousands of people each summer, who come to enjoy the physical and musical beauties, sit in the Big Shed or lie on the velvety lawns that extend from the opensided auditorium. The popularity of these concerts helped provide the money to support the school part of Tanglewood, the school that was so close to Koussevitsky's heart. The students are made up of instrumentalists, composers, conductors, and singers. Until Koussevitsky died in 1951, he taught the fledgling conductors.

The conductor is the only kind of musician who cannot do his practicing by himself. The student singer carries his voice with him, the instrumentalist owns his piano or violin, the composer has his pen and paper. But the conducting student cannot progress without steady access to his instrument, the orchestra.

The Tanglewood student orchestra was the Music Center's pride and joy, a group of 90 musicians, all in their teens and early 20's, individually very gifted and collectively of such high calibre that they soon began to be called the Junior Boston Symphony. The conducting students worked with them every morning under Koussevitsky's watchful eye, and on Friday evenings they would conduct a concert for the student body and public, each student conductor being assigned as many different kinds of pieces as the concentrated six-week session allowed him to conduct.

Directing most of the students' time toward intensive study of the inner life of music, Koussevitsky was also concerned with the external aspects in the training of a conductor.

He felt that correct podium deportment was an important asset to a conductor. He himself had a marvelously magnetic presence in front of an orchestra.

Just to see him come out of the wings and walk to the podium with that proud, sure gait of his produced in his audiences an electric excitement that pinpointed their concentration. They were ready for the music to come. Koussevitsky wanted his students to learn how to walk, how to bow, and in general how to comport themselves gracefully on the podium. To this end he hired a ballet master from the neighboring dance school, Jacob's Pillow, to give the students weekly lessons in what Koussevitsky called in an inimitable mixture of German and French, *"Die Plastique."*

Lenny went to the first of these lessons, and then he told Koussevitsky that he couldn't go again. Lenny felt that podium behavior must come naturally, from what the conductor feels; that to watch yourself in a mirror, one of the methods briefly used, could only lead to a self-consciousness that would inhibit and distort the conductors's instinctive technique.

Koussevitsky saw that Lenny was right, that it was unwise if not actually impossible to try to teach showmanship. The performer either has it or he hasn't. In any case, he shouldn't be made self-conscious about it. Lenny had it. He never had to think about his walk, his bow, or his conducting gestures. Whatever he did on the podium sprang from his direct response to the music, not from wondering how he looked while doing it. His podium deportment was never calculated or thought out. He conducted as he felt the music demanded. How a conductor looks to an audience depends on the temperament and innate style of the conductor, not on a learned set of gestures. The ballet master was dismissed.

During that first Tanglewood summer, it soon became apparent—to Koussevitsky, to the public, and to the local critics—that Lenny was *the* conducting student to watch. Though all the boys were gifted, some of them extremely so, Lenny stood out as special.

Soon he began to be special to Koussevitsky personally, too. He had no children, and Lenny became a kind of spiritual son to him. Lenny reminded him of himself when he had been young. Many people said they even resembled each other physically. Like a father, Koussevitsky wanted to pass on to Lenyushka, this student-son, his knowledge of and his love for music, to see his own talents live again in this boy with whom he felt such kinship.

All through the years until his death of leukemia in 1951, Koussevitsky and Lenny remained very close. The day before Koussevitsky died his wife called Lenny, who was then composing in Mexico. Lenny took the next flight to Boston and arrived at the hospital in time to spend the last evening of Koussevitsky's life beside him. They talked together late into the night. Unaware that he was about to die, Koussevitsky, the old conductor, spoke enthusiastically about his future plans for Tanglewood, about his plans for strengthening his already ardent support of contemporary music—and about his hopes for Lenny. It was a beautiful and wrenchingly sad night for Lenny. The next day Sergei Alexanch died. The musical world mourned the loss of one of their most admired and talented members. Lenny mourned the loss of his beloved teacher and second father.

Chapter **6**

Symphony No. 1

In the autumn of 1941, Lenny had been studying two winters with Reiner and two summers with Koussevitsky. Lenny was now ready—but for what? He was qualified to begin his conducting career—but where? During the next two years Lenny floundered.

He spent the first year in Boston. Koussevitsky had asked Lenny to assist him in weeding out new scores submitted to the maestro for performance. This work was not enough either to occupy Lenny's time fully or to give him enough money to support himself. Trying to solve both problems, Lenny decided to teach and advertised his intention in the local newspapers.

Nobody came. Well—one student came in from the suburbs to Lenny's Boston studio once a week for a piano lesson. And that was it. There was no pounding on the door by a host of eager pupils, just a knock by one brave soul.

Our father helped out, and somehow Lenny squeaked through the year, eating meagerly except for an occasional meal at home, composing but not showing the music to anyone—and trying to find hope for the future. Koussy asked him to learn the Chavez *Piano Concerto,* planning to schedule a performance later in the Symphony season. Lenny learned it but never played it. He had, with some difficulty, joined the musician's union earlier in that year so that he would be able to work professionally. Neither he nor Koussevitsky realized that his union membership would make him ineligible to play with the Boston Symphony Orchestra, at that time one of the few major orchestras in the United States that was still nonunion. The plans for Lenny's appearance with the orchestra were thus thoroughly quashed.

The bleakness of the year in Boston was temporarily relieved by the arrival in town of a Broadway-bound musical show in which Lenny's friend Adolph Green was appearing. The show was called *My Dear Public,* but the public evidently never got the message. It was a disastrous failure, closing with a grave-like finality in Boston. But during the two weeks it struggled along there, Lenny met and made a strong impression on Irving Caesar, the show's composer-lyricist, whose career went back to writing the lyrics for George Gershwin's first and greatest song hit, "Swanee" in 1918.

The following autumn, after a third summer at Tanglewood where Lenny was now assistant to Koussevitsky, Lenny once again and with great trepidation went to New York, jobless but determined. By chance, he ran into Irving Caesar, who not only remembered him kindly but did something about it. The main problem of the moment for Lenny was to find a way to support himself in New York. Irving Caesar sent Lenny to see Herman Starr, the president of Harms-Wittmark, a popular music publishing company. Lenny got his first job in New York.

His main duties were to listen to jazz records and write down the musical notation for the complicated improvised solo flights of the leading instrumentalists. This work was considered very useful at Harms Wittmark because no one else there was enough of a trained musician to transcribe onto sheet music what the ear heard on the record. Lenny also made piano transcriptions of popular songs for four hands and for eight hands on two pianos, for sixteen hands on four pianos, etc.

For all this work, which Lenny signed Lenny Amber, he was paid the less-than-princely sum of $25 a week. It wasn't enough to live on, but it was a start. Lenny earned some additional money by playing piano accompaniments at various ballet classes. The pseudonym Amber was a mild sort of joke; Bernstein in German means Amberstone.

Most of Lenny's free time was given over to the composition of his *First Symphony*, the *Jeremiah*. Lenny had decided to enter it in the New England Conservatory Competition for American Composers. All submissions to the contest had to be in by December 31, 1942. I came to New York from Mount Holyoke College on Christmas vacation and found Lenny up to his knees in manuscript, red-eyed from lack of sleep, racing against time to finish his symphony. He was still deep in the composing of the last of the three movements, the scoring was only half done, and there remained the tedious and time-consuming job of copying the whole work neatly and clearly. Only three days remained to accomplish all this before the deadline. It would take more than one pair of hands to bring it off. A small army of friends and I were put to work helping to get the mechanical part of the job done. I was kept busy inking in clefs and time signatures, two friends took turns making ink copies of the already completed orchestration, another checked the copies for accuracy, and Lenny's current girl friend kept us all supplied with coffee to keep us awake on this 36-hour, friend-in-need task.

While all this was going on, Lenny sat at a table in a corner of the room, finishing the actual composing. I suppose it was great training for his powers of concentration, but it was hard going for him to keep up the flow of creativity with the comings and goings all around him, punctuated with intermittent fits of giggling from his over-coffeed little band of helpers.

But somehow it all got done; and on December 31st, Lenny took the train to Boston, for it was then much too late to put the manuscript in the mails. He made it at the last minute, wearily tossing the score on the receptionist's desk at the New England Conservatory at five o'clock on the last day.

If this story were written for a movie, the fitting climax to such a dramatic, all-out effort would have Lenny winning the prize, the exhausted but victorious hero. In real life, there was no climax for Lenny, only an anticlimax. He didn't win. A composer named Gardner Read did, and he conducted his prizewinning *Second Symphony* in 1943 with the Boston Symphony Orchestra. Today he is professor of composition and music theory at the School of Fine and Applied Arts at Boston University. Lenny's entry, the *Jeremiah Symphony,* finally did win a prize two years later: the coveted New York Critics Music Prize for the best new composition heard that year.

Chapter 7

And God Said, "Take Bernstein"

Lenny's hectic effort to finish his *First Symphony* was over; the contest was unwon. Winter wore into spring that dark year of 1943; and Lenny's spirits sank lower and lower. There he was in New York, the center of music in America; but though he had met many kind people who liked him and were impressed by his talents, and though he was making a living—barely—the kind of work he was doing was light years away from the musical work he wanted to be doing. Here and there an opportunity threw a feeble light, but by summer the darkness had closed in again.

To make matters worse, there was no Tanglewood that year. It had become necessary to shut down the school and suspend the concerts for the duration of World War II.

Lenny felt utterly stuck and completely useless. He couldn't even be part of the War, as were millions of his contemporaries. He had been rejected by the Army at his first call-up in 1941. Lenny's childhood asthma had left its mark, making him, in the Army doctors' view, unfit for soldiering. Now in 1943 he was called for re-examination. This time, anxious to be accepted, he hoped to convince the examining doctors that since his asthma attacks only rarely recurred, he would be a good Army risk. But he got nowhere with the doctors; the head doctor was, of all things, an asthma specialist who categorically refused to consider Lenny as a recruit.

That night was a black one for Lenny. It seemed to him at that moment that life had thoroughly rejected him, even refusing him participation in his country's war.

The next morning, depressed beyond words, he left for Lenox, Massachusetts, where he was to assist Koussevitsky in a weekend series of lecture-recitals for the benefit of the Red Cross. It was the day before Lenny's 25th birthday. The coming year looked as bleak and forbidding as the one behind had been.

To try to cheer him up a little, I went to Lenox with him. That night he heard the first performance of his latest composition, the song cycle *I Hate Music*, and it helped a little. It was charmingly sung by Jennie Tourel, a mezzo-soprano whose success had been mainly in Europe and who was still three months away from a spectacular Town Hall appearance in New York.

Some time during that evening, Koussevitsky told Lenny that Artur Rodzinski, the newly appointed conductor of the New York Philharmonic, was looking for Lenny. Rodzinski was spending the summer on a farm near Stockbridge, a few miles away from Lenox. In search of Lenny, Rodzinski had called Koussevitsky but had said nothing beyond asking that Lenny call him. Lenny called; again Rodzinski said only that he wanted to see him. The next morning, still completely in the dark as to the purpose of the visit, Lenny went to Stockbridge and was met at the entrance to the Rodzinski farm by the conductor himself astride a motor scooter, wearing shorts and a bee-veil.

The two of them walked about the farm, perching finally on a haystack where Rodzinski talked about his search for the right person to assist him in his new post. He said he had considered all the likely candidates in the country, and for one reason or another he didn't want any of them. He had heard Lenny conduct the Tanglewood student orchestra a few times, and he had been impressed by him. In his indecision about choosing an assistant, Rodzinski said that he suddenly heard God say, "Take Bernstein."

An odd scene: sitting on a haystack on a sunlit August morning, facing a bee-veiled, distinguished conductor who invokes the name of God in giving his reasons for choosing you for a job. Lenny was thunderstruck. A man he had never before seen in his life had just handed him what was considered by aspiring musicians the plum of the year. When Lenny could find his tongue again, he blurted out his thanks to Rodzinski for trusting him with such a responsible position and soared back to Lenox on Cloud Nine, radiant with the surprise and excitement of his interview. His birthday was suddenly alight with promise and significance: his 25th birthday on August 25, 1943, the day his life changed so radically and happily. We went back to Boston that night in high spirits, a strong contrast to the melancholy and gloom that had hung over our ride up the day before.

Some people would call it God's intervention, others would call it Fate, Luck, Kismet, Destiny. Whatever name you give it, there does seem to have been at work in Lenny's life a force that goes beyond the limits of the conventional trials and opportunities in a young man's life. Lenny's doubts, his disappointments, his rejections, all seemed to have been part of the same path that led to his certainties, his achievements, and his success.

When Lenny's big chance came, it came with a rush. The Philharmonic season began in September with the new conductor Rodzinski on the podium. The equally new assistant was busy and happy, attending all rehearsals, going over new scores, studying old ones, and beginning to become a part of New York's musical life.

Only two months after he had settled into his one-room studio apartment in Carnegie Hall and was beginning to become familiar with his new job, something totally unexpected happened that put a swift end to quiet contentment, that put Lenny suddenly and explosively in the public eye. The opportunity was big and, fortunately, so was the talent that went to meet it, head on.

Chapter 8

Debut

The weekend of November 13, 1943 promised to be
an exciting one for Lenny. On Saturday night he was
to hear the first New York performance of his song
cycle, *I Hate Music,* to be sung again by Jennie Tourel
at her Town Hall recital. Our mother, father, and
twelve-year-old brother Burtie had come to New York
to share with Lenny what was up to that moment the
most important event in his professional life. That most
important event was to give way sharply and unforget-
tably for Lenny before the extraordinary happenings
of the following day.

The recital was a great success for Miss Tourel, with
a due share of applause going to Lennie as the composer
of the song cycle. The party given for them after the

recital was very gay and very late in ending. Lenny went sleepily home at four o'clock in the morning.

Five hours later the ringing of his telephone dragged him from sleep. It was Bruno Zirato, co-manager of the Philharmonic, with news that jolted Lenny wide awake.

"Lenny, you're going to conduct today's concert. Bruno Walter is sick."

Dr. Walter, who had been guest-conducting the orchestra that week, had fallen a victim to the flu virus that was making the rounds of New York that month. It had been hoped that he'd be well enough to conduct the Sunday afternoon concert, but his temperature was far too high for him to leave his room, much less conduct a strenuous two-hour concert.

Suddenly and startlingly, there it was. Only two months into his job as assistant conductor, Lenny was about to conduct his first Philharmonic concert in a sold-out Carnegie Hall, with millions more listening to the regular Sunday radio broadcast, everyone, of course, waiting eagerly to hear the great Bruno Walter. Luckily there wasn't much time for Lenny to brood over this astonishing and rather frightening situation. Since it was too late to round up all the men of the orchestra for a hurried, preconcert rehearsal, Dr. Walter had kindly offered to go over the program with Lenny.

Hastily throwing on some clothes, Lenny dashed over to the maestro's hotel. There for some two hours they pored over the music together. Dr. Walter gave Lenny some technical suggestions to help keep to a minimum the confusion certain to rise when the orchestra found itself being led by a conductor with whom they had never performed, with whom they had not even rehearsed the program.

The program of the day consisted of four pieces: Robert Schumann's *Manfred Overture;* a first-performance piece, *Theme and Variations,* by Miklos Rosza; Richard Wagner's *Meistersinger Prelude;* and, most difficult of all, Richard Strauss's *Don Quixote,* a long, highly complicated masterwork. This last was a special piece of Dr. Walter's. The only thing that gave Lenny any hope of being able to get himself and the orchestra through it without disaster was the realization that by chance he knew the piece much better than he might have known such an intricate and new to him work.

When he had been studying *Don Quixote* in preparation for Walter's rehearsals, he had become fascinated by it, spending much off-duty time at home studying it with the Cervantes novel on which Strauss based his orchestral composition, excited by the genius with which the composer had translated the pictorial and emotional essence of the novel into a stirring piece of music. Lenny clung to the hope that his long hours spent immersed in the score would help sustain him in conducting the music that day.

As the hours of the early afternoon began to fall away, Lenny dressed in his best suit and tried to study his scores. But it was impossible. The notes danced and skittered on the page. His nerves were too shaky for calm, last-minute perusal. He called our parents, who, unaware until that moment of their son's imminent debut, were about to drive home to Boston. Lenny said to our father, "You remember last night when I said you might have to wait ten years to see me conduct the Philharmonic? Well, you're going to see me do it today."

Next, Lenny got a message to Koussevitsky to listen on the radio, and then he went to the drugstore downstairs for a nerve-steadying cup of coffee. Next—but there was no next left except to head for Carnegie Hall backstage, early as it was.

Much of the concert itself remains today something of a blur to Lenny. He does remember the tension backstage before the concert began, the announcement to the audience that Dr. Walter was ill, the ensuing groan of disappointment, and then finally his walk to the podium, the polite applause, his hands lifting for the opening chords of the *Manfred Overture*. He also remembers that with those first three chords sounding full and strong and precise, his nerves steadied almost immediately; and he was able to give his full attention to the music.

The first half of the program seemed to go well, with the orchestra wonderfully cooperative and the audience responsive. At intermission, he fortunately had no time to worry over the huge work to come. The soloists featured in *Don Quixote,* a cellist and a violinist, came to his dressing room for a hurried conference. They had, of course, rehearsed with Dr. Walter, not

Lenny, and so it was vital to the simple cohesion of the performance that Lenny indicate to them what he planned to do. He indicated his plans as best he knew how.

Don Quixote takes about 35 minutes to play. They were 35 minutes of complete concentration for Lenny; he was deep in the music, the audience and his nerves forgotten. At the end of the piece, there was a moment of silence and then a roar of applause and shouting—the sounds of triumph. The ovation continued as a now thoroughly spent Lenny took bow after bow, acknowledging with unaffected amazement and delight the tribute from audience and orchestra.

Throughout the concert I had sat crouched by my radio in my dormitory room at school 300 miles from New York. I had been unable to join my family there for the weekend because I had to study for a series of upcoming exams. My father had called to tell me to listen on the radio. I gathered a few good friends around and settled down to listen. I remember it as a very frustrating afternoon. I didn't know the music to be played that day very well. What with that unfamiliarity, my nervousness for Lenny, and the fact the audience's applause was brought down low on the radio after each piece to allow the announcer's voice to be heard, I really didn't know if Lenny had done well or not, whether the concert had had some special impact or whether it had gone only passably well. My frustration was increased when I couldn't reach Lenny on the phone for hours. When I finally did, he was able to tell me only that the concert had gone far better than he could have expected, and that he was thrilled and exhausted from the experience.

What neither of us knew until the next day was that Lenny had become famous overnight. On Monday morning, the New York *Times* carried Olin Downes' review of the concert on the front page, using such words as "brilliant" and "exciting." There was also an editorial that said, "Mr. Bernstein had to have something approaching genius to make full use of his opportunity." The New York *Journal American* said, "One of the tests of quality is to possess it and produce it in an emergency. The result was acclaim for Bernstein." The New York *Daily News* editorialized: "It was like a shoestring catch in center field. Make it and you're a hero. Muff it and you're a dope. He made it."

Lenny's talent, the dramatic circumstances of his unexpected debut, and the vociferous audience response, all had made Lenny the hero of the moment; but much more importantly, his career had truly begun.

Chapter **9**

"Hats Off, Gentlemen, a Genius"

When I walked into Lenny's studio apartment five days after his explosive debut, I found one happy, slightly bewildered brother in a room overflowing with used flash bulbs and countless empty film boxes. The week had been crammed with interviews and picture taking. The telephone had rung constantly with requests and offers. Western Union messengers were practically a fixture at the door, delivering messages of praise and congratulations from friends, colleagues, and well-wishing strangers. Recognition and success were upon him. Opportunity had knocked, come in, and made itself at home.

From that week on, Lenny's career went into high gear and stayed there. The next 12 months were extraordinary ones indeed for Lenny.

No conductor of the Philharmonic had missed a performance in 15 years. Suddenly within two weeks, first Bruno Walter and then Howard Barlow fell ill, too ill to conduct. On November 27th, Lenny was on the podium again. This time he had more warning—even a rehearsal—and took the orchestra through Mr. Barlow's program with relative ease and an already fast crystallizing professional skill. One week later, Lenny was invited by Rodzinski to conduct one of his programs as a kind gesture of recognition from the maestro to his assistant. So, within one short month after his first appearance, Lenny led the orchestra twice more, learning a great deal from each performance, and each time adding to the strong favorable impression he had already made each time he stepped on the podium.

Artur Rodzinski

It was now clear to critics, colleagues, and audiences alike that the excitement caused by his debut was not a fluke, not an accident of circumstance, but that Lenny's conducting talents were genuine and impressive, backed up by solid training and knowledge.

In January of 1944, Lenny won public recognition for another aspect of his talents. Fritz Reiner, his old conducting teacher at Curtis, was now conductor of the Pittsburgh Symphony; and he had invited Lenny to conduct the premiere of his *Jeremiah Symphony*, the composition that had failed to win the composer's competition the year before. Reiner had seen the score, liked it, and wanted to give his former pupil the opportunity to conduct its first performance. So Lenny got a week's leave from his job at the Philharmonic to prepare for the premiere. Ironically, Rodzinski himself got sick that week while Lenny was away. William Steinberg substituted.

In Pittsburgh, after days of intensive hard work with the orchestra—the music was new and difficult for conductor and orchestra alike—Lenny conducted his symphony for the first time. Another old friend, Jennie Tourel, sang the vocal part of the "Lamentation" movement. She, the symphony, and Lennie were an enormous success. Once again Lenny found himself on the front page when a Pittsburg newspaper shifted its music review of the concert from its usual place on the inside pages. I don't know why the newspaper considered the concert important enough to report as a leading news event, but there was the headline: "BERN-STEIN SYMPHONY ACCORDED OVATION" The positive recognition that his *Jeremiah Symphony* received gave Lenny an even deeper happiness than the excited approval that greeted his conducting. He came back to New York a happy man and went back to work as assistant to Rodzinski. But the regular routine was soon broken again.

This time the Boston Symphony asked Lenny to guest-conduct and to include the Jeremiah Symphony on the program. The Boston newspapers didn't put their reviews of the concert on their front pages, but again he had great success, both as composer and conductor. The Boston *Post* music critic, Warren Storey Smith, said that he was "willing to go all overboard and quote Schumann's famous salutation to Chopin: 'Hats off, gentlemen, a genius!'" The fact that Boston was Lenny's home town, that his family and friends were there to hear him, that Koussevitsky beamed through it all—all of these things added an extra measure of sweetness to the heady elixir of success.

This time when Lenny got back to New York, he had to get down to concentrated work on an entirely new project that he had begun two months earlier. Jerome Robbins, a young and talented dancer in the Ballet Theater, was creating the dances for his very first ballet; and he had asked Lenny to write the music for it. There was little money in the project—Lenny and Jerry each got $300—but there was the opportunity and excitement of creating a ballet for the much admired Ballet Theater.

Lucia Chase, patron of Ballet Theater, believed in giving young and untried artists a chance. Jerry was only a character dancer in a company that boasted the presence of Alicia Markova and Anton Dolin, two great ballet stars; but Jerry's eagerness and confidence won Miss Chase over. The company was on tour for most of the time that Jerry was creating his ballet. He chose five other young dancers from the group—John Kriza, Harold Lang, Muriel Bentley, Janet Reed, and Shirley Eckl—and they worked on the ballet when they were not all traveling, rehearsing, or performing on the Ballet Theater's extended tour.

The collaboration between composer and choreographer was anything but orthodox. Lenny was guest-conducting all through that winter and early spring. He wrote the ballet score on trains, in hotel rooms, and in airports, wherever and whenever he could snatch the time away from the demands of his other commitments. Lenny and Jerry worked together by mail, telegram, telephone, and recordings. Long letters went back and forth, the budding choreographer detailing the story of three young sailors on a 24-hour leave in New York, describing the characters and moods of the ballet; the composer giving his ideas for the kind of music he thought would be right for the choreographer's ideas. Then Lenny would put the music he had composed on a record, adding spoken memos of explanation for Jerry.

[79]

These little records would go winging to the various cities on the ballet company's touring route, where Jerry would play them and create his choreography to fit the music. Back to Lenny would come another record with Jerry's suggestions for cuts, changes, and extensions. So it went for three months, at the end of which time the Ballet Theater returned to the city for its New York engagement.

On April 18, 1944, at the Metropolitan Opera House, the 25-minute ballet *Fancy Free* was performed for the first time. It was sandwiched between star-studded productions of *Swan Lake* and *The Nutcracker,* both long established classical ballets. No one expected much from this first effort by a completely unknown choreographer, six young dancers, and a relatively unknown composer, all of them in their twenty's. But from the first moment when the opening bars of a blues song sounded behind the still lowered curtain, the audience sensed an "event." Something special was about to happen. And happen it did.

As the curtain rises, the audience sees three sailors in spotless whites around a lamp post. Their gestures and dance movements show their hopes for a night on the town. One sailor rushes into a bar onstage, and the other two join him in drinking a glass of beer. A beautiful girl walks by and they chase off after her, showing off to get her attention. When the contest gets a little heated, the girl leaves and two of the sailors follow her. The third sailor starts sadly back into the bar, but he cheers up when he bumps into a girl and gets acquainted with her. They go into the bar, dance, and are just getting to know each other and have fun, when the other two sailors return with the first girl. It turns out that the two girls know each other; but two's company and three's a crowd, so the three sailors all dance in turn to see which two the girls will choose. Again the contest ends in a tussle, during which the girls sneak out. The sailors are right back where they started. Soon, however, another girl passes by and the sailors take off after her as the curtain falls.

The highly original, gay, rollicking *Fancy Free* sent the audience into paroxysms of approval. The six dancers, joined on the stage by the composer-conductor, received an ovation—they had to take 14 curtain calls—and the newspapers next morning were rapturous in their praise.

"To come right to the point, without any ifs, ands, and buts, *Fancy Free* is a smash hit," wrote John Martin, dance critic of the New York *Times*. "Fancy Free hit a whole row of jackpots," said another critic. Edwin Denby of the New York *Herald Tribune* called the new ballet "so big a hit that the young participants all looked a little dazed as they took their bows."

I had a tiny part of the triumph. Lenny had asked me to record the opening blues song. My pride at "being in" the ballet was tempered by the fact that Lenny had made me sing flat at the recording session, the better to simulate the style of current blues singers.

[81]

*Lenny and
Jerry Robbins, 1949*

Kubrick

Jerry Robbins became that night the outstanding new American choreographer, and Lenny's career as a composer for the theater was off to a brilliant start. Today *Fancy Free* has been performed more than 800 times; Jerry Robbins is one of America's most famous choreographers, acknowledged internationally as a major influence in the dance world.

Jerry and Lenny have continued their collaboration successfully. They did two more ballets together, *Facsimile* in 1946 and *The Age of Anxiety* in 1950. Facsimile tells the story in dance of a woman and two men at the beach. Alone, each does not know what to do with himself; together, as it turns out, they do not know either; so they part, capable only of acting out a copy of life. Lenny wrote *The Age of Anxiety*, his *Second Symphony*, in 1949 after reading W. H. Auden's long poem with the same title. The ballet tells in dance the story of four strangers, all anxious, who get some meagre comfort from an evening they spend together vainly trying to relieve their fears. They part at the end of the evening, each grateful to the others for the effort each has made to solve their common problem.

Jerry and Lenny also collaborated on two shows, *On the Town* in 1944 and *West Side Story* in 1957. *On the Town* was really an extension of the ballet *Fancy Free*. Again the three sailors are on 24-hour leave pursuing girls, but in *On the Town* they find them: a beauty queen, Miss Turnstiles; Hildy, a female taxi driver; and Claire, an anthropology expert. Like *Fancy Free*, *On the Town* was a great success, playing 463 performances. Of *West Side Story* we will hear more later. Both shows were made into highly successful motion pictures.

Lenny and Jerry's collaboration continues with a new show in the works, a musical version of Thornton Wilder's brilliant play, *The Skin of Our Teeth*.

Chapter 10

"*New York, New York, a Wonderful Town*"

A month after the *Fancy Free* premiere, the Philharmonic season ended. Lenny was not rehired as assistant conductor for the following year. Instead, he was
offered an engagement as one of the Philharmonic's
guest conductors in reward for his recent emergence
as a full-fledged conductor. He accepted happily, of
course, but he turned down most other offers to guest-
conduct other orchestras, and for a good reason.

The great success of *Fancy Free* had given Jerry
Robbins the idea of extending its story line into the
libretto of a Broadway musical, which turned out to be
On the Town. Lenny went to his friends Betty Comden
and Adolph Green, who were then performing in a New
York nightclub, and asked them to write the book and

lyrics for the show. When they accepted, the show was under way.

During the summer, Lenny had engagements to conduct several performances of *Fancy Free* in the Hollywood Bowl in California. Betty and Adolph went with him to the Coast; and it was on the journey out in their various train compartments that they really got to work on *On the Town*. Adolph and Betty not only did a great job on the book and lyrics; they also wrote two parts for themselves—Ozzie, one of the sailors; and Claire, the anthropólogy expert—which they played to perfection.

Betty, Adolph, and Lenny worked all summer on the show; but in the middle of the job, Lenny had to have an operation, which his doctors felt was necessary to relieve his chronic sinus infections. The operation was considered a minor one; and to insure the least loss of time because of Lenny's hospital stay, Adolph decided it would be a perfect time for him to have his own enlarged, infection-prone tonsils out. Lenny and Adolph look upon their operations together as a sort of gala affair.

Lenny went up to the operating room first and had an unexpectedly rough time. The local anesthetic chosen didn't work; he seemed to be immune to it. The attending doctors improvised various combinations, but nothing worked completely. The operation finally proceeded with Lenny only partially anesthetized. I saw him go by when he was wheeled down from the operating room, looking battered and exhausted. He was put to bed; and Adolph, who was ready to call the whole thing off after one look at his "operation mate," was taken up to surgery. As is usually the case with many tonsillectomies on adults, Adolph had great pain after his operation. A couple of hours later when Betty and I were allowed to visit them, we found two sick, wan-faced boys staring bleakly at us from their hospital beds. The lark they had planned to make of their hospital stay had begun very badly.

But in a couple of days they both began to feel better; and then, with Betty perched near their beds, they all three worked on the show. The floor nurses and patients in nearby rooms were alternately amused and irritated by the singing and laughter that erupted from Room 669. It sounded like a lot of fun—and it was—but it was also hard work. Once the boys were out of the hospital, the work really went into high gear. By October a rough version of the book, music, and lyrics was ready. The collaborators stood back and surveyed the situation. Six people were involved now: Lenny, Jerry, Adolph and Betty, and producers Oliver Smith and Paul Feigay—every one of them in their 20's, and none of them with any Broadway experience to speak of. They all decided that what was most needed was the direction and guidance of an expert, a Broadway veteran. With apprehension and humility, they played the score for George Abbott, producer and director of more than 20 Broadway shows. He was then 55 years old and one of the most respected and successful men in show business. He liked the score, took the script home to read, and to the ecstatic delight and surprise of the nervous sextet, he agreed to direct the show.

On the Town opened on Broadway on December 28, 1944, and was a big, big hit from the start. The year had come to a close—and what a year it had been for Lenny. He had made a brilliant beginning as a conductor, he had been recognized as a composer of superior talents, and he had written the music for his first ballet and for his first Broadway show. Everything had happened very quickly. There had been a great deal of hard work and a succession of dizzying successes. What there hadn't been was time for reflection. That time came now.

Problems arising from being an active composer *and* conductor had already begun to loom over Lenny troublingly. Lenny knew that two different roads of achievement lay open to him: in one direction, composing; in the other, conducting. He knew he couldn't, like the ubiquitous Lord Ronald of Stephen Leacock's *Nonsense Novels,* "ride madly off in all directions." Would he have to pick one part of the world of music in which to work, and stay there? Was it advisable, or even possible, to work in more than one part of that world at the same time? Now in 1944 began the conflict that has never really left him and that remains virtually unsolved today.

Chapter ***11***

The Complete Musician

In interviews down through the years, Lenny has
been asked over and over again: "Which will you give
up, composing or conducting? Can you give your best to
either when your attention is divided between the two?"

These questions Lenny asked himself at the beginning of 1945, and today he's still asking. In fact, answering the question has become progressively more
difficult. Since 1945, Lenny has added to rather than
subtracted from the number of his activities: he has
appeared often as a piano soloist; he has appeared on
television for more than eight years; he has written two
books—*Joy of Music* (1959) and *Leonard Bernstein's
Young People's Concerts for Reading and Listening*
(1962)—and he has taught conducting at Tanglewood,

and served as director of the School of Creative Arts at Brandeis University. And last, but far from least as we shall see later, he is very involved in a full family life built around his wife and three children.

The solution to the problem, if there is one, is elusive. He's tried it every which way. At one point, he gave up conducting for two years in favor of full-time composing; at another time, he stopped all composing and concentrated solely on conducting. He's tried doing them together. That approach usually results in articles about him with such titles as "Is Bernstein Spreading Himself Too Thin?"

Let's see if for once the true facts and emotions surrounding this important aspect of Lenny's life can be discussed clearly and without prejudice.

First of all, Lenny has always had many talents. As a boy, in addition to his multiple musical gifts, he wrote both prose and poetry passably well, and he even painted a little. Many things came easily to him. His enthusiasm, his ability to digest what he was learning, and his powers of concentration have always been high, whether he was studying philosophy or learning how to dive. As he grew up, this power and ease became even more firmly set in him.

At the age of 25, when he first became well known both as a conductor and composer, Lenny was first confronted with frowns of opposition from various quarters of the musical world. Some people frowned on one activity, and some frowned on another. To the con-

sternation and confusion of some of those frowners,
Lenny didn't fit at all into the tradition of the conductor's way of life. It is an ancient tradition and a very
conservative one. Conductors have been almost without
exception—Gustav Mahler was a big exception—just
that, conductors. It's true that here and there a conductor may also transcribe pieces for symphony orchestra,
a conductor may teach, or a conductor manage to fit
into his schedule operatic as well as concert conducting.
But for the most part, a successful maestro follows a
carefully laid out routine from which he rarely departs.
This routine consists of rehearsals, performances, recording dates, constant studying of scores—old and new—
careful diet, and plenty of rest. Conducting is a demanding art, and conductors mostly live well ordered lives.

Until Lenny arrived on the scene, an American had
never really been taken seriously in the conducting
world. It was as if America's distrust of her own
cultural level had made her reject any native-son can-
didate for a place in the thoroughly Europeanized world
of conducting.

Then along came this young American, younger by
20 years than the youngest of his colleagues, his talents
unmistakable as he burst onto the musical scene with
a force that could not be ignored. His youth and the
exuberance that went with it disconcerted many a tradi-
tion-bound symphony board member. Accustomed to the
older, more formal European conductor, they were
unprepared for the arrival in their midst of a wholly

different breed of conductor, one who was distinctly a product of his own country and time.

For instance, Lenny's love for and participation in the popular musical theater jarred and even shocked some of the people in the loftier positions of the concert world. It meant that he would have to break new ground, create a new atmosphere for acceptance if he were to convince the more staid people that his enthusiasm for the popular kind of music was his natural inheritance, not something to be condemned as beneath a concert conductor's interest.

It has been hard for some to accept a maestro who also composes symphonies, writes for Broadway, and is a prominent television personality. Lenny is something of a maverick, and the realization of this has created uneasiness in many quarters. In the 20 years after 1943, that unease in some measure abated. As proof, in 1958 Lenny was offered and accepted a seven-year contract as musical director of the New York Philharmonic-Symphony Society, the longest running contract ever given to a conductor with that institution.

But, of course, even that hasn't solved the basic problems of the conducting-composing conflict. Time is one of those problems; energy is another. In his mid-40's, even Lenny's extraordinary energies aren't what they were in his mid-20's. Division of interests is another problem. Some critics argue that when Lenny accepts a post as a conductor, he must do that and nothing else. Any other arrangement, they conclude, cheats the public of the best he can give them. I don't agree with this argument; but the critics have long tradition on their side, and I have only my own convictions on mine.

Lenny is sometimes written and talked about as if his own deepest feelings were of little consequence, as if the main point at issue were to get him to conform to an image already conceived for him. Maybe that's the way it unavoidably is once you become "public property."

But what *about* Lenny? What are the qualities in him that make him need to work in more than one kind of music, that refuse to allow him to choose just one and to be happy with it?

The Lenny that most people know, the Lenny that is "on view," is a warm, gregarious man, quick to laugh, highly knowledgeable, articulate, and confident. These are the qualities that take over when he is being the performer—the conductor, the pianist, the television teacher.

The less well-known side of Lenny is in many ways another sort of man. He is no longer so much the performer, the doer, but a man who will sit for hours hovering over a half-filled page of manuscript paper, trying to find the next phrase of the music he is writing. In his composing periods, Lenny becomes decidedly quieter, more brooding, a little withdrawn from his fellows, less drawn to the world of pleasure and activity. It is a lonely time; but as all creative artists know, the loneliness is an essential part of the creativity. When an artist has to "make something up" by himself—whether it is a piece of music, a novel, or a painting—if it's to be any good, he must draw that something from the innermost parts of himself, his most deeply rooted feelings and thoughts. That drawing out can be an immensely difficult business, sometimes depressing, and always a thoroughly exhausting and lonely process.

To the casual eye, it looks to be a fine thing, a present from the gods, to have as many talents as Lenny has. And of course it is in many ways. But to find the means to fulfill these talents to their highest potential is not easily done.

There is, on the one hand, a great advantage for Lenny by being a composer as well as a conductor. On the podium when he is at his best, he is able to identify with the composer of the music he is playing, to feel as close to the piece as if he had written it himself. The disadvantage, on the other hand, comes when he is composing. His head is so full of other people's music, all the varied kinds of music he's been conducting, that the difficult enough process of composing becomes that much harder. He must make an enormous effort to clear his head of the thousands upon thousands of notes he has been studying as a conductor, in order to find his own notes, his own music.

Both sides of Lenny—the performer and the creator—are strong in him. When he deliberately denies one side and gives all his attention to the other for any long period, he is the less for it. He's using only half himself. Contrary to the people who say he must choose, I believe that each of his talents feeds the other and makes him the better artist. Rather than choose, I would hope for him that he will find the road that leads to him doing *all* the things he most wants to do, even if the way gets blocked, even if there are, temporarily, bypaths and detours.

Chapter 12

Promise Unfulfilled

After his first full year of conducting and composing successes, Lenny was besieged with offers of all kinds, ranging from an offer to star in motion pictures to an invitation to become the conductor of the newly formed New York City Symphony. The second invitation, he accepted; to the first, he said, "No thanks." But a polite refusal didn't do the trick right away. The motion picture company insisted that he at least consider the offer. The proposed film was to be a biography of the Russian composer, Petr Ilich Tchaikovsky, and the big lure was the promise of the great Greta Garbo to play Tchaikovsky's noble patroness and friend, Madame von Meck. With the mention of Garbo's name, Lenny's cries of "Ridiculous! I'm not an actor." quieted to a dazed whimper. He had always adored Garbo in the movies. The idea of even meeting her, much less becoming her costar, gave him a dizzying moment or two. Taking advantage of his momentarily star-struck condition, the producers made him promise to make a test for the movie. Before he knew what was happening, Lenny found himself studying a scene to be played before the camera in a couple of days. I helped him study the lines. Most of the study time was spent roaring helplessly with laughter over the silliness of the writing and the spectacle of Lenny's trying to take the whole thing seriously enough to say the lines with a straight face. It was a terribly written scene, and Lenny's acting was equally terrible.

When I saw the scene in the projection room, for the first three minutes or so I was rather impressed. The scene began with Lenny sitting at the piano, playing very well and looking marvelous. Then he started to speak his lines.

I think that in order to be a really good actor, you need, besides a talent for acting, a decided lack of humor about yourself. Lenny had neither of these requirements. He didn't have the acting talent, and he was far too quick to see the ridiculous side of himself to be able to take the attempt seriously.

That was the end of Lenny and the movies. Now something truly close to his heart was demanding his time and attention, the New York City Symphony. Made up exclusively of young players, it had just come

Lenny rehearsing the New York City Symphony, 1945

into being. It bore the city's name but it was actually falsely named. Although the public was encouraged to think that New York City funds supported the orchestra, the truth of the matter was that no money at all was contributed toward its support by the City. The players received woefully small salaries, and Lenny took none at all. But still, somehow or other, they managed to put on a short ten-week series of concerts for three seasons, each concert being looked forward to with high anticipation by the young and enthusiastic audiences, audiences utterly unlike the much bigger, richer, and less responsive patrons of the New York Philharmonic concerts.

The City Symphony audiences came to expect, and got, unusual programs built around new pieces, long neglected, interesting old ones, and seldom played masterpieces. The audiences heard such compositions as Bela Bartok's *Music for Strings, Percussion, and Celesta,* a masterwork that had caused great excitement in the 1930's when it was first played and then had lain neglected; Aaron Copland's *Piano Concerto* from the 1920's; Beethoven's *String Quartet in A Minor* as transcribed for full string orchestra by Dimitri Mitropoulos; Sibelius' seldom played *Fifth Symphony;* the premiere of Marc Blitzstein's *Airborne Symphony;* Darius Milhaud's seldom performed *Concerto for Two Pianos;* and Igor Stravinsky's oratorio-opera *Oedipus Rex* from the 1920's.

Working with this orchestra was very rewarding for Lenny, not in a financial sense, but artistically and emotionally. He and the players were all young. Learning and achieving together, becoming finer artists together was exciting and gratifying. Olin Downes wrote in the New York *Times* of the opening concert in 1945, "The young musicians were with their leader heart and soul, and it was gorgeous to feel the fire and pulse of their playing." At the end of the season, Howard Taubman of the *Times*, summed up, "New York City Symphony concerts at the City Center remain among the most stimulating and agreeable events in town."

But the perilous financial situation of the orchestra did not improve. At the end of three years, funds from the City were still not forthcoming despite all the pleading that Lenny and others did. Ironically, appeals to the usual alternate source of support—the public— were forbidden. The name of the orchestra and the hall in which it played, New York City Center, implied a City-supported institution, and the authorities didn't want that implication to be lost. Lenny would have been able to continue heading the orchestra without salary because of his income from guest-conducting and pay-ments from his ballets and shows. But it was an impossible situation for the orchestra players. Ten weeks work at an average of $40 a week was hardly enough money for them to live on. When it became painfully clear that the season could not be extended, and that salaries could not be raised, Lenny resigned with great sadness. The New York City Symphony soon passed out of existence.

Until after World War II, Americans who were at all culture-conscious felt that their own country was distressingly inferior to the major countries of Europe in the performance and appreciation of all the arts. This feeling had grown partly out of the fact that in Europe the arts and the artists had for hundreds of years been established and respected as an important part of a nation's natural wealth. The United States, less than 200 years old, had had neither the time nor the inclination to encourage or to make much of its artists. This fact, coupled with the general European delight in calling attention to the culturally "barbaric Americans," had resulted in our having become over-awed by European culture and under-appreciative of our own. What we had lost sight of, and what Europeans had very little idea of, was that America had first-class talent of her own in all the arts—not just great jazz and Ernest Hemingway. With the ending of World War II, Europe began to see some of that talent.

Lenny's first visit abroad was to London in 1946. The four-week trip was anything but a success. Everything went wrong from first to last. Less than a year after the ending of the War, the English were weak from six long years of too little food, too little sleep, too little warmth, and too much bombing. Lenny found an orchestra understandably without much spirit, tired, not even able to play in tune. He hated the programs he had to play, programs that had been dictated by contract. The orchestra management had insisted on Edvard Grieg, Tchaikovsky, and Richard Strauss.

Unprepared for the cold of London, Lenny had brought all the wrong clothes. Since he didn't have any of the necessary clothing ration coupons, he was unable to buy even so much as a warm scarf. Chilled to the bone day and night, he eventually fell ill and had to cancel a whole group of concerts. In a letter to me he wrote, "Of all things I came down with a strep throat this week. Leinsdorf had to substitute for *me!* There's a switch." All in all, his first trip to London was not a happy time.

The following spring he was to make his first trip to continental Europe. He conducted over a period of three months in France, Italy, Belgium, the Netherlands, Czechoslovakia—and in Palestine. He was very excited about the trip, if a little apprehensive, especially after the ill-starred experience in London. The various European orchestras had never been conducted by an American. Lenny was warned that they were likely to be highly suspicious of him. The general feeling among them was that America couldn't produce a genuine, well trained maestro who really knew music. Instrumentalists who had played under the batons of such great European-born conductors as the Hungarian Arthur Nikisch, the Dutch Willem Mengelberg, the German Wilhelm Furtwängler, the Italian Arturo Toscanini, and the Russian Koussevitsky were bound to look warily upon a 28-year-old American.

Duly warned, Lenny was still very excited about his first look at the Continent. So was I—because I was going too.

Chapter *13*

Promise and Fulfillment

We were true innocents abroad. Even the hotel we chose in Paris showed how little we knew. In our childhood we had both been very impressed by a star-filled movie called *Grand Hotel;* so we stayed at the Grand Hotel in Paris. It was enormous, dank, cold, and bleak. Our first evening, just off the boat, we scanned and rejected a pitiful menu sent up by room service. In a city famous for its fine food, we ate our first dinner of roast chicken out of cans and we drank instant coffee, all of which we had brought with us. In all fairness, I have to admit that this was only a year and a half after the War; good food was scarce even in the best hotels. But even granting the dire lack of creature comforts in postwar France, the Grand Hotel was a dismal place for such eager, first-time-in-Paris travelers as we were.

Our attention quickly shifted to a matter far more important than great food and pleasant surroundings. We were supposed to leave for Palestine in three days, and we still lacked the necessary visas permitting us to land in Egypt. The only air route from Paris to Palestine at that time involved a quick change of planes at the Cairo airport. It soon became clear that everything would be done to make it as difficult as possible for us to fly in and out of Egypt. A visit to the Egyptian Embassy brought only a smooth but steely announcement from the vice-consul: "We have had instructions from Cairo *not* to issue you visas." Just like that. The reasons for his behavior weren't hard to figure out: we were Jewish, Lenny was well-known as a partisan of the Zionist cause favoring independence for Palestine as well as for his music; and it suited the Egyptian authorities to make his entry into Palestine difficult if not impossible. Our travel agent told us that the only other way to go was by a Greek ship. The voyage would take nine days and the ship had rats as well as passengers aboard. Lenny's first rehearsal with the Palestine orchestra was scheduled to take place in three days. If that date could could not be met, there was no point in going at all.

An appeal to the American Embassy had brought sympathetic but vague answers from the harassed officials. Hundreds of bewildered American travelers were milling around the Embassy asking for various kinds of help. It looked as if we were not going to get to Palestine. We were frustrated and depressed.

Then, with a last surge of energy, the day before our scheduled flight (there wasn't to be another for a week), we went once again to the American Embassy. This time we were luckier. One of the officials was a fan of Lenny's, which increased his concern with our problem. In less than an hour a formal note in French went around to the Egyptian Embassy stating that the American Embassy would be most pleased if visas were issued allowing us to land in Cairo. Like magic, if with a certain amount of grumpiness, we got them. We were off.

But our little cold war with the Egyptians wasn't quite over. We arrived at the Cairo airport the next morning at seven. Our connecting plane, on the Egyptian line called the Misr Airwork, left at nine. It wasn't to be that simple. From the moment the man in customs began supposedly checking us through, we sensed trouble. He announced to us that the connecting plane was small; so we would have to leave all our luggage behind for them to send on later. Agreeing to that plan clearly was saying a final good-bye to all our belongings. The likelihood of our ever seeing them again was mighty small. The atmosphere was tense and hostile. We were about ready to count ourselves lucky to lose our luggage and get *ourselves* out of Egypt when the customs inspector's position shifted. He finally ruled that the matter could be arranged with a $300 payment for "overweight baggage," in addition to the "gift" of Lenny's fountain pen, which the inspector had been eying throughout our negotiations.

[*107*]

Fifteen minutes later we found ourselves tucked into our seats on a nine-passenger, one-engine plane, the aisle of which was piled to the ceiling with passengers' luggage, which also barricaded the washroom door. The pilot revved up the motors with the cockpit door wide open while casually puffing a cigarette. We averted our eyes in horror, clutched the coats and other loose luggage stacked on our laps—and hoped for the best. An hour and a half later, we landed safely at Lydda Airport outside Tel Aviv, unbelieving but thankful that we were actually there.

Palestine was one year away from becoming the independent nation of Israel. It was still British mandated territory and governed as such. But Palestinian underground groups such as the Haganah and the Irgun had become very active, reflecting the country's urgent wish to become independent. It was a time of what were referred to as "incidents": a British diplomat kidnapped, a power station blown up, a threat to the governor-general. As a result, an eight o'clock curfew had been established; for two months there had been no evening entertainment, no strolling in the streets after dark.

For Lenny's concerts the curfew was lifted. Audiences jammed into the overflowing halls, and they reacted to the music with an excitement I've never seen equaled in any other country. Lenny conducted there for three weeks, moving up and down the small country, playing in the cities and in the kibbutzim, the communal farms where everyone lives and works together, sharing the profits.

All the audiences were extraordinary, listening to the music with pinpoint concentration, and at the end applauding and shouting with an electrifying intensity that grew even more fervent with each concert, as if they were trying to communicate to the conductor their approval of him and their joy in the music he was making for them. They communicated all right. For Lenny, the whole experience in Palestine with the orchestra, the audiences, and the people he met was one of the most moving times of his life.

One night when he was conducting in the outdoor amphitheater of a kibbutz, the electric lights suddenly went off. We were told the power failure was likely due to Arab sabotage. This kibbutz adjoined the Jordanian border and had been victims of such sabotage before. The amphitheater was packed with people who had come from as far as 50 miles away to hear the concert, come on horseback, on burro, and on foot, feeling their way in the darkness, slipping under barbed wire—all to hear a concert. In the face of their effort, power failure or not, the concert could not be called off. The audience sat quietly in the dark for two hours waiting for the auxiliary generator of the kibbutz to build up enough power to provide the necessary lights. At ten-thirty the lights finally came on again, and Lenny began the concert.

The ties between the people of this country and Lenny grew and remained very strong. The next year he returned to a Palestine-become-Israel. He found the country in the middle of an out-and-out war with five Arab nations, all of whom had attacked the newborn state as soon as it had achieved its independence from the British. One would think that in the midst of such a battle for its life, there would be little time for, or interest in, such things as listening to music. And yet again the concert halls overflowed with eager, music-hungry audiences, many of them now in uniform.

One day Lenny asked for volunteers from the orchestra to go with him to Beersheba to play for the soldiers, who had captured it from the Egyptians only the day before. Twenty-five men, their instruments, and Lenny were loaded in a bus and driven to the front lines. As the word passed along to the troops that there was going to be a concert for them, thousands of soldiers began heading for the place chosen for the concert, which was really only a large hole in the ground, the site of an archaeological excavation.

Israeli intelligence officers later told Lenny that Egyptian reconnaissance planes, flying high over the area and seeing this mass movement of troops proceeding on foot, reported to their superiors that Israeli forces were converging on a given point, from which place the Egyptians assumed that the Israeli would launch an attack. The Egyptians accordingly made preparations to meet an attack stemming from Beersheba. It never occurred to the Egyptians, of course, that in the midst of the war, all those soldiers were heading for a concert, not a battle.

As it turned out, there *was* an Israeli attack that day, but in a region far away from Beersheba; and the Egyptians were not prepared to meet it. The intelligence officers told Lenny that this miscalculation on the part of the Egyptians made a big difference in the ensuing course of the war. Lenny was sure that the importance of the incident was exaggerated for his benefit, but the story made him feel good anyway.

Since that year Lenny has been back to Israel three times. Despite a firm resolve he has made not to do any guest-conducting while he is the conductor of the New York Philharmonic, he plans to return to Israel once again to conduct their orchestra. Such is the devotion he feels toward the people of that extraordinary little country.

Chapter *14*

Music, Travel, and Henry

In every city, as we traveled from place to place on that first European tour, Lenny's first rehearsal would be marked by curiosity, suspicion, and, to some degree, resistance on the part of the orchestra. The warnings he had received before we left America were proved correct. Conducting was felt to be a uniquely European talent. Since no American had ever become an internationally known and respected conductor, musical Europe assumed it couldn't be done, that the New World simply wasn't cultured enough to produce one. This prejudice that the various orchestras brought with them to their first rehearsal with Lenny was only strengthened when they saw facing them on the podium not only an American, but a rather informal and a very young one.

It was fascinating to watch the change in the men from the first day's rehearsal to the next. The first surprise was that Lenny was able to talk directly to them, not through an interpreter. Lenny has always had a gift for languages. At that time he spoke good French, fair German, and passable Italian. Even with a language as outlandish to the English-oriented ear as Czech, he managed to learn enough words and phrases to establish some communication with the Prague Orchestra. As we will soon see, it would have been well if he had been fluent in Czech.

The second biggest surprise for the players in the orchestras was that Lenny knew what he was doing, that he was a skilled and trained musician with a deeply personal approach to music that gave the players a fresh interest in pieces they'd been playing most of their lives and an attentive respect for the less familiar works on the program. At the first rehearsal, inevitably, the men addressed Lenny coolly as "Mr. Bernstein"; at the second rehearsal, their greeting was an admiring and warm "Maestro."

The reactions of audiences and critics in every city were everything Lenny could have hoped for, ranging from pleased to ecstatic.

One of the most exciting parts of the tour was the visit to Milan. There Lenny had the privilege of conducting at La Scala, probably the most famous and surely the most beautiful opera house in the world. (Lenny wasn't conducting opera this time—that was to come five years later when he conducted a performance of *Medea* starring Maria Callas in the title role.)

The main work of this debut symphonic program at La Scala was Gustav Mahler's gigantic *Second Symphony*. Now, in Italy opera is loved and sung by everyone. Cabdrivers are likely to be heard whistling part of a Puccini aria, and cleaning women humming the "hit tunes" from *Rigoletto*. But symphonic music is much less well known in Italy. As for the Austrian composer Mahler, incredibly only the most musically sophisticated people in Italy had even heard of him, much less listened to his music.

Although his *Second Symphony* was completely unfamiliar to most of the Scala audience, it nevertheless scored an enormous success. After the concert, backstage, a lady came up to Lenny, a nice lady, a local patroness of the arts. She complimented him warmly on the performance and then with complete innocence she said, "How pleased and gratified your friend Mr. Mahler must be to have you play his music so beautifully." Since she had never heard of Mahler before, she could only assume he had just appeared on the musical scene, never dreaming that he had died some seven years before Lenny was born. Lenny was hard put to it to answer her. Rather than embarrass her by correcting her mistake, he thanked her for her praise and let it go at that.

This incident was the first example, in exaggerated form, of something we were to find often as we made our way around Europe. It gave us great pleasure to realize that America was not at all the artistically backward country we had been told we were for so many years. In many arts—not only in music—we found that American audiences generally knew more and that our artists were producing at a higher creative level than in Europe.

After the debut concert at La Scala, a reception was given in Lenny's honor. It was all very formal and grand, everyone in evening dress, the rooms and decor elegant as they could be. The guests, including the lady who thought Mahler was a friend of Lenny's, blinked in disbelief during the party as from time to time they caught sight of an 11-week-old dachshund skittering along the marbled floor. They weren't seeing things—it was my puppy Henry, bought in the south of France two weeks before.

During the concert he had been left all evening alone in my hotel room. After the concert, hating to leave him alone a minute longer, Lenny and I had stopped off quickly at the hotel and picked him up. We had found him in a corner of the room crying piteously, but as soon as he saw us he perked up, and he behaved beautifully at the party. He padded contentedly about the rooms, happily picking up crumbs that dropped from the guests' plates. Luckily our hosts loved dogs and understood perfectly.

I suppose it seems a little bit crazy to travel all over Europe with a tiny puppy. We were lucky in that dachshunds (or at least this particular dachshund) seem to love to travel, settling down happily in planes, trains, and boats, or lying quietly at your feet under the table during dinner.

One dinner involving Henry neither Lenny nor I will ever forget, a dinner in Paris at the superelegant home of the superelegant Marie-Blanche, Comtesse de Polignac. Lenny had asked our hostess if we might bring Henry, thinking we could leave him in the kitchen during dinner. But Marie-Blanche wouldn't hear of leaving him in the kitchen. She also had a dachshund and knew how miserable they were when they were away from their owners. So under the table Henry lay, while liveried servants came and went, serving and taking away through out two-hour dinner.

On my right sat François Valéry, an official in the French government and son of the poet Paul Valéry.

Henry, Lenny, and Shirley

At the end of the meal, when he rose from the table, he stared aghast at his bare right foot. Two hours earlier he had had a black silk sock there. It had been delicately but thoroughly unraveled and chewed by tiny, teething, sweet little Henry. No wonder he had been so quiet throughout the dinner. He had had a marvelously amusing toy to play with—François's sock. Thanks to the warm graciousness of our hostess and to François's sense of humor, the incident became an occasion for hilarity instead of the terrible embarrassment it could have been.

Henry helped provide distraction and fun for Lenny on the tour to help relax him after the very hard work he was doing. Every ten days we were in a new city, he was facing a new orchestra, rehearsing a new program, and struggling with a new language. But all of it was exciting.

An International Music Festival was being held in Prague. Lenny, who had conducted there the year before, had been invited as guest conductor from America. Many countries were represented at the Festival. France was represented by Charles Munch, who later came to the United States as conductor of the Boston Symphony. Rafael Kubelik, one of the two Czech conductors, later served as conductor of the Chicago Symphony Orchestra.

This year of 1947 was the second year since 1939 that Czechoslovakia was being governed by Czechs. In the year to come they would be taken over by Russia, and behind them lay six years of German occupation. When Lenny began rehearsals for his concert in Prague, he ran into the still violent feelings of the Czechs about anything German. He had programmed a Bach *Brandenburg Concerto;* he was told that after six years of enforced listening to practically nothing but German music, the Czechs weren't quite rational on the subject. German music, whether it was Bach or Wagner, symbolized to them the hated German occupation. To make matters worse, German was the only language in which Lenny could communicate fluently with the orchestra, managers, taxi drivers, hotel people, and wellwishers. As a result, there was constant tension. He solved the programming dispute by substituting Aaron Copland's *Symphony No. 3* for the Bach and playing the dramatic overture *Husitská* by the Czech composer, Antonin Dvorak.

Russia was represented at the Festival by conductor Eugene Mravinsky of the Leningrad Symphony, composer Dimitri Shostakovitch, and violinist David Oistrach. We met the Russians only once, backstage after a fine Mravinsky concert. It was impossible to exchange more than surface pleasantries with them, since one was made uncomfortably aware of a group of other Russians who hovered nearby—men, one deduced, assigned to watch the musicians.

As I listened to the brief exchange of amenities between Lenny and Mravinsky, the Russian conductor

At Chopin's piano

Japanese friend   *Solo at La Paz, Bolivia*

At Honolulu

*Rehearsal
in Venice*

[121]

impressed me as a charming, warm, highly civilized man.

Shostakovich was something else again. As he stood there, stiff and tense, stuttering as he spoke a few words in Russian, it was clear that he was an inordinately shy, severely nervous man, uncomfortable to the point of fainting at finding himself faced with a room full of strangers. He soon walked away from the little circle, while Mravinsky continued to talk to Lenny. Mravinsky said he would very much like to have Lenny come to Leningrad to conduct, and that he himself would very much like to come to America to conduct the New York City Symphony, which was then Lenny's orchestra. Lenny agreed that such an exchange would be wonderful but that the way the world was, such invitations would have to come from their respective governments. Both conductors would have to wait a long time.

It wasn't until 12 years later in 1959 that Lenny went with the New York Philharmonic to Russia as part of the American-Russian cultural exchange plan, sponsored by the United States State Department. As for Mravinsky, he had to wait until October of 1962 to make his first and highly successful appearance in America with his Leningrad Symphony.

I went to Europe with Lenny again in 1950. This time our younger brother Burtie went too. Burtie was then 18, a sophomore at Dartmouth College—and a great companion. The three of us have always had fun together; we enjoy each other and take pleasure in being together. So the month spent in Europe, traveling to England, the Netherlands, Germany, Ireland, and France, was filled with high spirits and much laughter. A lot of that laughter came from a temporary obsession with which we were all three afflicted—the card game, canasta. We played it everywhere, on the move in planes and trains, settled into hotels, or visiting as guests in a castle in Ireland.

On many nights, when the concert was over and our backstage greetings were made, we would dash back to our hotel, order some food, and continue our mad canasta tournament.

I guess the height of our madness was reached in a game between Lenny and Burtie, which they played in

Lenny, Shirley, and Burtie

a car taking us from Shannon Airport in Ireland to our hotel. As we drew up at the entrance of the hotel, I got out of the car and looked back, staring in disbelief at my brothers. Oblivious to the fact that we had arrived, the two of them sat on in the back seat, surrounded by luggage, melded cards stuck into any convenient part of the upholstery, intent only on finishing their wild game. I hesitate to think what the driver of the car and the doorman of the hotel made of us. Crazy Americans!

Besides making out very well at canasta, Lenny scored a great professional success on the tour. Orchestras, audiences, and critics were all warmly receptive; he was accepted and hailed everywhere as an authentic first-class maestro.

Lenny has returned to Europe many times since then; he has traveled to South America and to the Orient, becoming finally an internationally acclaimed man of music.

Chapter *15*

"O Happy Birthday, Dear Daddy-O"

Felicia and Lenny met each other in 1946, became engaged, and then became unengaged. They met again in 1951, and this time they were sure they wanted to be married to each other.

Felicia Montealegre Cohn was born in Costa Rica to a Chilean mother and an American father. Roy Elwood Cohn, her father, became president of the American Smelting and Refining Company works in Santiago, Chile, where Felicia and her two sisters grew up. The Cohns visited the United States often when the girls were small, going most often to San Francisco where most of Mr. Cohn's family lived. Felicia was bilingual from infancy, being able to read and speak English as easily as Spanish. When she reached the age of 21, she had the legal choice of becoming a Chilean or United States citizen. She chose the United States.

In her teens, Felicia had decided that she wanted to be an actress. At home she was an active leader in community theater. That was considered a proper pastime for well brought-up girls in Santiago. But any mention of becoming a professional actress was met with frowns of disapproval. So Felicia found another way. She had been studying piano for many years and was considered good enough to be taken seriously by her parents when she asked to be allowed to come to New York to continue her studies with the distinguished pianist, a fellow Chilean, Claudio Arrau.

When she arrived in New York in 1946, she took a couple of token lessons from Arrau, but she spent most of her time studying acting. During the next few years she began appearing on television. By the time she and Lenny were married in 1951, she was one of the most successful actresses in the medium. Using the name Felicia Montealegre, she appeared in leading roles on such programs as *Studio One, Kraft Theater, Philco Theater, Armstrong Theater,* and *Omnibus.* In 1949 she won the *Motion Picture Daily* Critics Award as the best new actress of the year.

The July weekend that Felicia and Lenny decided to get married ended in a happy celebration but began in great confusion. Lenny was at Tanglewood teaching and conducting when Felicia returned to New York from a three-month stay in Europe. I set out at 8:30

on a horribly hot, humid morning to meet her boat. I watched for her to come through customs for what at first seemed to be hours and in fact finally turned out to *be* hours. By 11:30 there wasn't a soul left except me, melting on the pier, waiting for a nonappearing Felicia. Puzzled and weary, I went home to find all of Felicia's luggage piled in my living room. She had left a short, plaintive note about my having forgotten to meet her, and telling me that she had taken the morning train to Tanglewood to see Lenny.

I felt awful about the meeting mixup. It's dreadful to come home after a long time away and not have anyone there to welcome you back. Unable to reach Lenny, I finally borrowed a friend's car and drove for three and a half hours to Tanglewood. Disheveled and sticky with the heat, I burst into the dining room of the inn where Lenny was living—and there they were. They stared at me balefully, sure that my hectic ride from New York was intended as an atonement for having forgotten to meet the boat that morning. But by the time Felicia and I had exchanged stories and realized how narrowly but surely we had missed each other, first at the pier and then at my apartment, the whole thing had become funny and calm was restored.

By the end of the weekend, Lenny and Felicia had decided to get married. And so they were, in Boston on September 8, 1951. Felicia looked beautiful and nervous; Lenny looked handsome and nervous. Right after the wedding they drove to Mexico, where they planned to live for a year. Lenny wanted to take off at least one season from conducting and devote all his time to composing. During this stay in Mexico, he wrote most of his one-act opera, *Trouble in Tahiti,* which does not have a tropical setting, as you might suppose, but tells of the bickering of a married couple in the suburbs. The title comes from that of a movie the wife has seen. The premiere performance of the opera was given in June of 1952 at the Festival of Creative Arts at Brandeis University.

In the late summer of that year, Lenny and Felicia came back to New York, intent on finding an apartment quickly because they were about to have a baby. Jamie was that baby, a peach-skinned, golden-haired little girl. Since she was the first new baby in the family, she was the object of constant wonder. We would all stand around her bassinet for hours, excitedly calling attention to her every little movement and sound, as if no baby had ever before lifted her head and given an angelic smile to the doting adults hanging over her.

Lenny and Felicia have had two more babies, Alexander in 1955 and Nina in 1962. All three are beautiful children, the older two bright and sensitive and a joy to be with, and Nina a cuddly, delicious dumpling of an infant.

Many people ask Lenny if the children are musically talented. Up to this point, neither Jamie nor Alexander has shown any inclination toward a serious study of music. Jamie has taken piano lessons for two years, but she is no different from 99 per cent of all young piano students—she doesn't want to practice. She is enormously musical, though; she sings in a sweet, true voice, and from time to time she busies herself with making up little songs.

I think that having music going on around you all the time, hearing your family play it, going to concerts at the age of four, all this gives a child the sense that music is a natural-as-breathing, everyday part of life, not the makings of a special occasion. Music must be for Jamie and Alexander as candy is for the children of a candy-store owner: they never have to hunger for it; it's always available to them.

Listening to music is as natural for Lenny's children as looking at trees or hearing a bird sing. It's a constant and pleasurable part of life to them, and I'm sure that their pleasure will grow as they do.

Jamie and Alexander are very proud of their father, and they have some realization of how well-known he is; but they are both beautifully unbrattish about it. The day after one of Lenny's televised young people's concerts, Jamie was telling me about children at school clustering about her, telling her what fans they were of her father's. When I asked Jamie how that made her feel, she said, "It makes me feel very proud deep down inside, but in a way that makes me not want to boast of it."

Love flows naturally and warmly between Lenny and his children. They have great fun together, whether

Piano for six hands

Margery Lewis: The Saturday Evening Post

On the pier

Avedon

Haircut

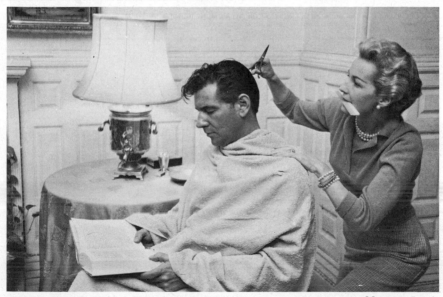

Margery Lewis

[131]

they're playing scrub baseball in the country, a game
of canasta (Jamie and Alexander are both whizzes at
it), or just sitting around quietly, talking together.
When Lenny is with the children, he is completely with
them, giving them all his attention and energy. A lot of
affectionate teasing and nonsense goes on. The children are at ease with their father, and they show it.

Last summer, Lenny returned from Europe a few
days before his birthday. For a week the children had
been preparing a show in honor of the occasion. It
was enchanting, with topical sketches, songs, imitations
—even specially written television commercials.

The closing number was a birthday song with
lyrics by Jamie, set to a tune from a current Broadway
show, sung by both children with gusto and warmest
feeling. Some of the words went like this:

"O happy birthday, dear Daddy-O,
I guess that Life just doesn't go so slow;
'Cause you are already forty-four years old,
But you can conduct, and you can compose, and you
*   can still be bold.*

> *Way down deep in your heart*
> *You're not growing old;*
> *So listen to our words:*
> *Happy birthday,*
> *Happy birthday*
> *Daddy-O."*

Chapter *16*

Music for the Theater

Wheii you look at the list of Lenny's compositions on Pages 188-192, you see that except for one piece, *Sonata for Clarinet and Piano,* composed way back in 1941, everything he has written relates to or springs from a specific idea, a story, an existing piece of prose or poetry, or a specific emotional attitude. He has written no music which relates only to itself, its notes, its structure—what is known as abstract music. For instance, when he began to compose some short, light, unrelated pieces titled *Five Pieces for Brass Instruments,* he ended up by making them very much related. Each of the five is named for and was inspired by a particular dog he had known and been fond of. One piece is called "Elegy for Mippy I," the first of three marvelous

[*133*]

mongrel pets that the family had with the same name; another, "Fanfare for Bima," is related to Koussevitsky's spaniel; and a third, "Rondo for Lifey," to a terrier belonging to his friend Judy Holliday.

Lenny's second symphony, *The Age of Anxiety*, was inspired, as we have seen, by the long poem of the same title by W. H. Auden. About *Serenade*, his latest big symphonic work, although he disclaims any literal "musical story," Lenny says in his program notes: ". . . it resulted from a rereading of Plato's charming dialogue, The Symposium. The music, like the dialogue, is a series of related statements in praise of love."

When he is composing, Lenny seems to like best working with a central idea, a unifying theme, something that to him gives the work a "spine"; more abstract composers find a satisfactory enough "spine" in the shape of the music itself, as in the classic sonata form, the three-movement concerto, the one-movement tone poem. As a conductor, Lenny can be excited by the most abstract, formalistic pure music, but as a composer he is drawn to write music that springs from a literary or emotional idea.

Composing for the theater, therefore, has been a very natural form for Lenny to work in. From this first show, *On the Town*, to his fourth, and most recent *West Side Story*, his shows have had a highly personal stamp on them. His scores are, all of them, unmistakably Bernstein scores. This kind of hallmark is an important characteristic of a real show composer. Because Lenny is a trained, serious musician, he is one of those rare birds in the theater, a composer who can write and score his own ballet music. His shows sound all-of-a-piece because the musical style is coming from one head— his. Most show composers write their songs and then someone else puts the various tunes together to make the overture, the between-scenes music, the ballets, and everything else that is required for the complete score.

Composing the score for a show usually takes about a year. Two of Lenny's shows had unusual and completely opposite histories in regard to the length of time it took for him to finish them. *Wonderful Town* took 5 weeks. *Candide* took three years.

Wonderful Town was adapted from the play *My Sister Eileen,* which in turn was based on a series of *New Yorker* stories by Ruth McKenny about two sisters who come to New York to become an actress and a writer. They have a series of hilarious adventures as they pursue their careers. A composer had been hired to do the score and Rosalind Russell was signed to play the lead. Five weeks before rehearsals were to begin, the director, George Abbott, who had so ably directed Lenny and Jerry Robbins' *On the Town,* heard the complete score for the first time and felt that it wasn't right. The problem immediately facing him and the producers was Miss Russell. If they postponed the show for a season, they would be likely to lose her as the star. She was free from movie commitments for only a certain length of time; and it was in that time, and only then, that she could do the show.

Mr. Abbott called Lenny for help. Would he take on the job of fixing up the score? Lenny felt that he couldn't do that—patch up another man's work—but then he had a rather bizarre idea. Outside of a few concerts, the following couple of months would be fairly free for him. If Betty Comden and Adolph Green, with whom he had done *On the Town*, were also free and would agree to work with him, how about the three of them writing a completely new score and lyrics for the show? Mr. Abbott was overjoyed at the suggestion, but his long experience in the theater made him question anyone's ability to do an entire musical score of any value in five weeks. Lenny conferred with Betty and Adolph; the three of them questioned their sanity to think that such a thing could be done. Then they took a long, deep breath and went at it.

For the next five weeks they worked 18 hours a day, shut away in Lenny's dark, gloomy studio—dark and gloomy perhaps, but evidently the right, closed-in atmosphere that they had for the work that needed to be done.

I remember many an evening during these weeks when I visited with Felicia. We would be sitting chatting in the living room, not far from the closed door of the studio. There would be no sign of the threesome, only an occasional concerted shriek of laughter and the sound of the piano dimly heard. Late in the evening, the maid would knock on the door and go in, bearing coffee or some food for the marathon workers.

Six weeks later, right on schedule, *Wonderful Town* went into rehearsal with its brand new score. The show opened in February of 1953 to rave reviews and had a highly successful run for a year and a half. It had been a long shot, but they had won.

Though Lenny, in his heart, never thought he had written anything like as brilliant a score as many re-

Rosalind Russell in Wonderful Town

United Press International

viewers thought it to be, he was enormously pleased at the results of the five gruelling weeks of work on *Wonderful Town*; and he was grateful that it had all come off successfully.

None of the songs from *Wonderful Town* made the hit parade, but then Lenny's songs rarely do. People in the "pop music" business tell Lenny that his songs are too hard, too unwhistleable, the voice range is too exacting for nonprofessionals to cope with easily. These comments have always puzzled Lenny, and once or twice he has deliberately tried to write an "easy" song, hoping to find the formula for a hit tune—but the songs weren't very good. From there on in, he's just forgotten about "how to write a song hit in 32 easy bars" and written his songs as they came to him, dictated by the needs of the show, not by his wistful wish for a song hit.

One song in *Wonderful Town* did have a certain popularity for awhile, and that was ironic. The song was called "Ohio." When Lenny, Betty, and Adolph wrote it, they thought of it as a spoof song, a sort of takeoff on songs of nostalgia about one's home state. They thought it obviously a joke-song; but to their surprise and amusement, it was taken seriously and sung as a straight up-and-down sentimental song. Well, that's show business.

As fast as *Wonderful Town* was written and put on Broadway, just as slowly did it take *Candide* to get born and make its appearance.

This show was a completely different kind of effort. The basic material was the classic novel *Candide,* written by one of the great literary figures of all time, Voltaire. The dramatist whose task it was to adapt this masterwork was one of America's most talented and honored playwrights, Lillian Hellman. The show was to be directed by one of the world's most distinguished stage directors, the British Tyrone Guthrie, later Sir Tyrone. The lyricist was Richard Wilbur, one of the best known serious poets in the country. Lenny had always been a great admirer of Lillian Hellman. They met in 1949, and after that his admiration for her as an artist was heightened by his personal affection for her. They had talked often of doing a show together. For Miss Hellman, a writer of strong drama, the idea of collaborating on a musical was appealing and challenging. She had told Lenny she would like to do an operetta kind of a show, perhaps based on a classic novel or play. Among the works that had come up from time to time for consideration and discussion were Lord Byron's long poem *Don Juan* and George Bernard Shaw's *Arms and the Man* (on which had already been based the Oscar Straus operetta *The Chocolate Soldier*). Lenny and Lillian had finally decided on Voltaire's *Candide,* thinking to find in it fertile material for a show abounding in song, satire, and spectacle. Voltaire's satirical philosophical novel tells the story of a young man, Candide, who has been taught by his tutor Dr. Pangloss that this is the best of all possible worlds. Candide sets out from his native

Westphalia with his sweetheart Cunegonde to test this optimistic philosophy, and as they travel to Lisbon, Paris, and Buenos Aires they suffer every possible kind of disaster. The book ends with Candide and Cunegonde back in Westphalia willing to cultivate their own garden instead of worrying about the world.

There was trouble from the beginning with this show. The brilliant novel did not lend itself easily to adaptation for the stage, even under the experienced and talented hands of Lillian Hellman. Then, the right lyricist was hard to find. By the time they were through, Richard Wilbur, Dorothy Parker, and John La-Touche had all written lyrics for the show, and here and there even Lenny and Lillian had contributed a few. The adage about too many cooks spoiling the broth isn't true only in the kitchen—it applies in the theater, too.

After the show opened in Boston, it was clear to all concerned that *Candide* was in trouble. In the three weeks before the New York opening, everyone did all that could be done to try to fix it; but they were hampered by lack of time, a seemingly unworkable basic story, and major errors made at the beginning that couldn't be undone in the short time at hand. Sifting together the proper ingredients in the exact amounts to arrive at a show that is really good and a hit too is a tricky, elusive job at best. The collaborators on *Candide* made mistakes, enough of them so that the show wasn't either a truly good show or a successful one.

Candide ran in New York for only 73 perform-

ances, about two months, a run that, of course, puts it
definitely in the flop category. Yet there was enough of
the stirring and beautiful about it to elicit great praise
from the critics for some parts of it, while most critics
agreed that the show as a whole didn't work.

As for Lenny's work in it, many critics, colleagues,
and just plain listeners think *Candide* is the best theater
score he has yet written. In the years after it opened on
Broadway, there were many offers from various sources
to revive the show, from opera companies and from off-
Broadway producers. In 1958 a concert version toured
the country successfully; the original-cast album had an
unusual success for an unsuccessful Broadway musical,
selling more than 45,000 albums.

But these somewhat comforting statistics aside,
Candide was a failure, Lenny's first commercial failure.
For someone who is used to winning all the time, losing
can come as a rude shock. It's no fun to work very
hard at something for three years and then fail with
it. Lenny's reaction to this failure was no exception.

But he recovered quickly. In the first place, it is not
in Lenny's nature to sit feeling sorry for himself for
long; and in the second place, he was already deep in
work on a new show.

Some six years earlier, in 1952, Jerry Robbins had
come to Lenny with an idea for a musical, a kind òf
New York version of *Romeo and Juliet,* in which Shakespeare's Montagues and Capulets would be translated

into 20th century Manhattan Monticellis and Kaplans. In other words, Jerry wanted to use Shakespeare's basic story of a young girl and boy in love, who are kept apart by families that hate each other. He wanted to set this situation in New York on the lower East Side where there are clusters of racial and religious groups in the same area living very close to each other physically but sometimes worlds apart in customs, beliefs, and prejudices.

Jerry, Lenny, and playwright Arthur Laurents met several times to discuss the show they temporarily called *East Side Story*. But somehow the ideas didn't come easily, the meetings weren't going well. A couple of months later, recognizing that, for whatever reasons, the show wasn't taking shape as they had hoped it would, they stopped work on it and each of them went his separate way.

Four years later Lenny and Arthur met by chance in Hollywood and fell to talking about the show they didn't do. An hour later they were deep in a discussion of the new social element that had taken root in New York since they had talked last. Puerto Ricans had come to New York in great numbers; there had been a steady increase in clashes between the newcomers' teenage gangs and the already existent gangs of other peoples in the poorer sections of the city.

The dramatic possibilities of such a situation, put in the framework of the *Romeo and Juliet* story, began to excite Arthur and Lenny. When they returned to New

[*142*]

York, they met again with Jerry; and out of this meeting came the first solid ideas for the show that was to be retitled *West Side Story*.

Many people thought that the three of them were crazy to write a musical for Broadway about juvenile delinquency, racial antagonisms, and a love story that ends tragically. The "people who knew" said that it could never be a hit. But the three collaborators turned deaf ears to the discouragers. Lenny, Arthur, and Jerry wanted the show to be a hit, of course, but they knew that if they worried about that and deliberately tried to follow what was considered the success formula—lots of tunes, beautiful girls, gorgeous scenery, happy ending—then they wouldn't write the show that they

Carol Lawrence leads West Side Story *dancers*

United Press International

had all envisioned and in which they believed.

There are people in the theater, as in every other profession, who are so frightened of failure that they prefer to stick close to the already accepted kind of show, with no attempt at new approaches. That Lenny went straight to work on a show commonly considered to be commercially a risky venture right after the failure of another risky venture is one of the reasons I like him.

Exactly contrary to the way that the various elements in *Candide* had *not* meshed, with *West Side Story* everything fell into place beautifully. The dancing, the music, the story, the performances—from the opening gang rumble to the closing tragic moments—everything combined to charge the show with a vitality and intensity that held the audience rooted to their seats.

The show opened in September, 1957, less than a year after the opening of *Candide*. This time, there were no ifs, ands or buts—*West Side Story* was a smash hit. It was a hit in London, too, where *Candide* had the same mixed reception that it had had in the United States. The motion picture version of *West Side Story*, released in 1961, won the second largest number of Academy Award Oscars of any picture in the history of the awards. Oscars went to George Chakiris and Rita Moreno as best supporting actor and actress, and other awards were won for production, art direction and cinematography in a color film, costume design, film editing, music scoring, and sound.

Six days after *West Side Story* opened on Broadway, an exhausted but happy Lenny was back on the podium in Tel Aviv, Israel, conducting the opening concert in the newly built hall of the Israel Philharmonic Orchestra.

The next week after that Lenny was back in New York to begin his first season as joint conductor, with Dimitri Mitropoulos, of the New York Philharmonic. The theater would have to be forgotten for awhile. It was conducting time again.

Chapter 17

Lenny and the Philharmonic

Lenny's relationship with the Philharmonic is a unique one. There is a kind of family spirit between them that I don't believe exists between any other major symphony orchestra and its conductor. This relationship didn't come about all by itself; it took many years and several adjustments and readjustments on both sides.

When Lenny first met the men of the orchestra, he was the assistant to Arthur Rodzinski and was 25 years old. In the first years of his leading them as an invited guest conductor, he was still pretty much in the position of "the kid who made good." But in 1957, when Lenny shared the directorship of the orchestra with Dimitri Mitropoulos, there began to be changes. After one year of joint directorship with Mitropoulos, Lenny became the sole permanent conductor of the orchestra.

[*147*]

Dimitri
Mitropoulos

From the point of view of the men in the orchestra, Lenny was now their boss, with the authority to discipline, hire, and fire them. From Lenny's point of view, this orchestra was now his responsibility. He had to make the transition with them from being a young guest conductor to becoming the mature permanent conductor in full control of his orchestra. The head of an orchestra is in part the "Daddy," the one to whom the men come when troubled or in need of help. Assuming that role takes a bit of doing when you are younger than many of the men you have to be "Daddy" to.

Lenny thinks that there was a specific turning point in his musical and personal relationship with the orchestra. They were rehearsing Mendelssohn's *Italian*

Symphony one morning in 1958. The orchestral parts were all marked up from many years of rehearsals with as many different conductors. Each conductor has his own ideas about how the piece should go: phrasing, dynamics (how loud or how soft a passage should be), tone colors, and other musical matters. The *Italian Symphony* had been played so often over the years that the orchestra took it for granted and played it almost automatically. Lenny spent the entire rehearsal that morning taking the first movement apart, having the men erase all the confusingly different penciled-in markings, and rehearsing the first movement from the first bar as if they had never played it before. For the first half hour of this rehearsal, there was some ill concealed grumbling from the orchestra. They felt that they could play the piece in their sleep. Why all this "unnecessary" work?

But as the rehearsal progressed, just as a piece of beautiful silver comes back to life when the tarnish is carefully removed, bit by bit the first movement of the symphony began to come shiny and clear again. After working most of the morning with them on the first movement, Lenny conducted it through from beginning to end. It sounded so marvelous and new that after the last note had sounded, the men burst into spontaneous applause.

That session, Lenny feels, was the turning point between him and the Philharmonic, the time when a mutual respect and admiration took solid root. Lenny

[*149*]

Lenny at Work

On television

Roy Stevens: The Philharmonic-Symphony Society

Young People's Concert

CBS Television

Recording with Jenny Tourel

Don Hunstein, Columbia Records

[151]

really became their conductor that day, but the new seriousness and solidity of their relationship didn't alter the camaraderie and family feeling between them. All the members of the orchestra still call their conductor Lenny. (It's hard to imagine orchestras addressing Stowkowsky as Leopold or Ormandy as Eugene, let alone Leo or Gene.) Lenny has helped men in the orchestra solve many of their personal problems, whether it's

Shostakovich takes a bow, Moscow, 1959

been finding a doctor for one of them or making a loan in time of financial need. Both Lenny and the Philharmonic have gone far together in more ways than one.

Besides the many many concerts given in New York each season, at Carnegie Hall, since 1962 at the new Lincoln Center, and in summer at Lewisohn Stadium, they have toured all over the United States and through most of South America and Europe. They have

Backstage in Moscow, 1959

had great success wherever they have gone, whether to Des Moines, Iowa; Istanbul, Turkey; Caracas, Venezuela; or Moscow in the Union of Soviet Socialist Republics.

Lenny has tried several innovations during his tenure with the Philharmonic. One of the biggest departures from tradition was his decision in 1960 to make each Thursday night concert—the first one of each week —a preview, asking the critics to come on Friday afternoon instead. The reason for this change was to allow Lenny to talk informally to the audience each week. The season's programs were built around central unifying themes: A Survey of American Music; Past, Present, and Future; The French Approach in Music; The

[*154*]

Middle European Approach; and so forth. Each week there would be at least one piece on the program that would tie in with the current central theme, and Lenny would talk to the audience about it.

This was a pretty radical move in the tradition-heavy concert world. Why did Lenny do it then? Because he believes that too often concert audiences just sit there listening passively, letting the music wash over them without really listening to it. He feels that if he can give them an idea of what to listen for, a point of reference, if he can provoke them into active listening, he may help to achieve something he feels most deeply about—bringing music of all kinds nearer to the people, bringing the people closer to music.

This has been the goal of his work on television, too, another aspect of Lenny's career, one that began in 1954.

Lenny first appeared on television for 33 minutes on a live telecast of Omnibus, a Sunday afternoon "intellectual" hour-and-a-half show. For 25 of those 33 minutes, Lenny examined and analyzed the first movement of Beethoven's Fifth Symphony, playing excerpts from the composer's sketchbooks, which contained rejected versions of the great symphony. Lenny showed the audience how Beethoven finally arrived at the version we all know, giving at the same time some indication of the agonies of indecision and torment of spirit that the composer had to pass through before he was able to

[155]

complete composing the movement. The last eight minutes, he examined and analyzed the first movement first movement, conducted by Lenny.

To everyone's great surprise and delight, there was a big positive reaction to the show, and not only from the television critics and music lovers. The wonder of the response was that it evoked an unlooked for interest in "just people" through all parts of the country, people for whom music had been suddenly made more meaningful.

This performance on Omnibus was followed by "What is Jazz?" and "The Art of Conducting." In 1955, the entire hour-and-a-half program was given over to an exploration of American musical comedy. Lenny has done more than 30 shows on television, all planned, written, and executed by him.

In 1957 he began televising the Young People's Concerts. They have become amazingly popular across the country with children *and* their parents. I say "amazingly" because serious music on television doesn't usually attract many viewers. Lenny loves doing the Young People's Concerts. Many of his friends have suggested that he drop some of his television shows since they demand so much in time and energy. He has cut down on television work, but not on the Young People's Concerts. He feels strongly about helping young people to understand and love serious music, in the hope that it may become a natural part of their lives and not the closed mystery it is for so many of their elders.

There's no question but that he has helped. He has the wonderful ability to re-listen with young ears to the music he wants to present, to listen as if he had never heard the music before. He can think about music freshly because his curiosity about it never deserts him. This quality, as well as his inventiveness and the ease with which he communicates his ideas, and most important of all, his respect for and understanding of young people, make these concerts interesting, instructive, and fun.

I think what is perhaps most significant about Lenny and television is that he has been able to bridge the gap between the strictly limited audience of educational television and the larger audience of entertainment television. Because of his ability to reach both kinds of audiences, he has been able to make music more immediately understandable and more exciting to hundreds of thousands of people who might otherwise have missed the experience of such music. In this way television has helped Lenny to make come true for him, in large measure, his wish to help people know what he knows, the joy of music.

Chapter 18

"I Write a Letter to You for First Time"

No matter how well qualified I may feel I am to sum up, to evaluate Leonard Bernstein, the musician, and Lenny, the man, I'm afraid my judgments would be suspect, open to accusations of bias, family loyalty, and lack of objectivity.

I think I *can,* though, be allowed to tell you how nice it is to have Lenny as a brother and friend. For all his formidable talents, I would admire and like him far less were he not seriously dedicated in his work and personally a thoroughly nice guy. Like all brothers, he can sometimes go too far in teasing, or behave with something less than the soul of tact; but he is kind when kindness is needed, and always fun to be with, whether we are laboring over a brain-contorting English crossword puzzle, making a home movie, or playing water volleyball.

As for his impact as a musician, I will let Lenny's audience tell you about that. Lenny has received many thousands of letters from people of all ages in every part of the United States and abroad, people from every conceivable station in life. Helen Coates, Lenny's secretary, keeps all these letters carefully filed. I reached blindly into this staggering collection of letters and pulled out at random a bunch from the years 1959 through 1961. I chose one over another in respect to variety of expression, age of the writer, and geographical location. The range of these letter writers makes the old nursery counting-out rhyme: "Rich man, poor man, beggar man, thief, doctor, lawyer, Indian chief," sound like a very restricted list.

I shall let these letter writers tell you how they feel about Lenny. Some of them are most extravagant in their praise, but they give a better idea than I ever could of the success Lenny has had in bringing music to the people of America. None of the letter writers knows Lenny personally, but only through his concerts, compositions, and television appearances. This—with all their individuality of spelling, capitalization, and expression—is what they say:

"Dear Mr. Bernstein,
   "My name is Diana Star King, and I am fourteen years old. I have wanted to write you, but I could not

think of how to put down on paper what I wanted to say. I finally decided to just sit down and write, and see what came out. So, here it is.

"Up until a few weeks ago I sincerely thought that the only good music was jazz or rock and roll. Then one Saturday morning I casually turned on the television set. On the first station I came to, one of your Young People's Concerts was showing. I decided I might as well watch it. I watched the entire show, and enjoyed it more than anything I can remember.

"Since then I have seen more of these concerts, and also a program on Sunday which you conducted.

"My parents feel that I have finally awakened to what good music really is, but I feel that this is not totally true. I had listened to symphonies ect. before, but I never enjoyed them. I think it is through you, the way you explain the music and tell how it works, in the gentle easy way you use that I have finally discovered good music. I am going to continue to watch you, and I am sure that I will grow to understand music better.

"I would be very happy if you could send me a picture of yourself, and if you ever have time, (I know you are a very busy man) would you drop me a short note. I sure would like it. I like you more than all the movie, and record stars put together.

Your friend,
Diana Star King"

[*161*]

At the Young
People's Concert

This letter, written on paper that is very prettily bordered with pink butterflies and blue flowers, is typical of a great many letters Lenny has received; but it shows, perhaps, an unusually individual perception of the process of really getting to know music. (She got her picture.)

A great many letter writers make a point of the fact that while they are not chronologically young, they are eager listeners to the Young People's Concerts. Such is the letter from Mrs. Norton B. Crane of Goldenrod, Florida. She says:

"You can't know how much those Young Peoples Concerts have meant to us—and the Sunday one. And we are not all young people! My mother is 76 and wears a hearing aid, so she can't go to the Florida Symphony Concerts with the rest of us. But with the aid of a gadget called a 'Magna-Mat' she can thrill to the music you and your friends play. The Symphony concerts are so

much more meaningful to me and my 22 year old son
and 13 year old daughter since we have had your in-
comparable descriptions and explanations. I can't use
words like you do to tell you how we feel—just thank
you, thank you!"

It is amazing how many of Lenny's television audience are psychologically young, however old in years.
One such is Mrs. Clara L. Leer of the Bronx, who wrote:

"At five minutes after the hour of one, with the
pulse of that stirring waltz still beating in my mind, I
hasten to write you my thanks for today's concert.
"At the age of sixty-four I am one of the 'children'
in that vast T.V. audience who gained better understanding of what to seek for, or how to let any music speak to
you.
"Some of the younger ones seemed to find the hour
a bit long for them, but I feel sure that it was one that
those like myself, who heard are so happy we tuned in
for, and will eagerly await the next of the series.
"Thanks, Many Many thanks!"

Some of the older "young people" seem as stirred
as the young in years, such as Mrs. John P. Briggs of
Rocky River, Ohio.

"Do you have any idea what is happening to we
dormant, musically retarded adults that are watching

[163]

your Saturday program? Can you possibly imagine
what can happen to someone who finds himself exposed
to an understanding and an interpretation like never
before?

"I am 36 years old and short of Dr. Damrosch didn't
find much to inspire me in the small Wisconsin town I
grew up in. True, if I ever had had much talent, that
wouldn't have stopped me. However, it is we ordinary
folks that I am speaking of. Ordinary talent-wise, that
is.

" . . . I hope you know what a stirring up you are
giving we poor, ordinary mortals and how fortunate we
feel to be able to listen to you for the far-too-few times
that we have. We rank beginners that have suddenly
discovered what we are missing and now must make up
for all that lost time. I don't know whether to compare
you to the Pied Piper or Billy Graham. Each has his
effect and you surely have yours!"

A lady from Arcadia, California, showed perhaps
the greatest youth range for listeners:

"I am a little girl of 65 and I loved your children's
concert this morning. My daughter 37 loved it, my
grand daughter 10 loved it, and our dog Tippie age 1
loved it."

From Walla Walla, Washington, came a letter em-
phasizing again how Lenny's television appearances

[*164*]

awaken interest in live concerts at home. A. J. N. Martin wrote, enclosing clippings about the celebration of the golden jubilee of the Walla Walla Symphony Orchestra and the Walla Walla Symphony Society and the Pink Champagne Ball held as a benefit to raise funds for the orchestra. She wrote:

"This may seem presumptuous but I can't resist telling you how enchanted we of Walla Walla are with your thrilling, glorious orchestra performances over T.V. Even my husband, who knows little about music, remarked after some of your 'youth concerts,' 'Dumb as I am about music, I am fascinated by these concerts.'

"We aren't all cowboys or Indians as the 'Westerns' picture us, as you may see by these clippings.

"Oh! for more lovely music on our programs."

For many people in smaller cities, attending live concerts is difficult or impossible. Mrs. Emery Lancaster Pierson of Lancaster Lands, La Grange, Missouri, wrote:

"You really cannot know how many people, particularly those in small towns, depend upon and appreciate your Saturday morning programs for children. They are truly superb and I feel of great value, not only to me, but to my small daughters.

"However—Saturday (March 8) I couldn't get a picture, and while we could hear you, it wasn't the same to the little girls. I was completely frustrated and in my frustration an idea was born.

"Would it be possible for you to have a film made of your programs?"

Letters came to Lenny in all shapes and sizes, most of them handwritten, but occasionally on business stationery, like the letter of Berel Caesar, attorney at law in Philadelphia, whose crisp-looking, electric-type-writer-produced letter runs as follows:

"I am writing you on behalf of my son, Neil, age four.

"Neil has been a fan of yours since he was two as a result of seeing one of your television programs. Since that time he has been inspired to learn the instruments of the orchestra and is generally interested in good music.

"While driving the other day we tuned to our local classical music station when Neil inquired, 'How come Mr. Bonestein doesn't come on any more?' We advised him that you were off for the summer and asked why he wanted to know. His reply, 'He is my friend.'"

From the chambers of Senior United States Circuit Judge (Sixth Circuit) Florence Ellinwood Allen, came the following handwritten note:

"We should, of course, thank the Ford Motor Co. for sponsoring your fine programs. But most of all we should thank you, who create them.

"The comparison and differentiation of the Sophocles and the Stravinsky was superb."

[The orchestra had performed Igor Stravinsky's *Oedipus Rex,* based on the tragedy by Sophocles.]

One of Lenny's most interesting letters came from Japan from Yoshikazu Kubo, who not only asked for, and got, a photograph of Lenny, but sent one of himself. He wrote:

"I write a letter to you for first time.

"I beg your pardon for my unskilful sentens.

"I'm now 18 years old and student of Keio University and one of the classic music fans in Japan.

"We have on two radio stations every Saturday noon and Wednesday evening a hour and half hour radio concert of the New York Philharmonic Orchestra.

"I always heard the N.Y. Phil's concert on Far East Network in leisure time.

"For Example [and he listed 45 programs with conductor, program and soloists, to which he added] Etc.

"For my taste, N.Y. Phil Orch. is not only the best in America but also the best in the world.

"I especially favorite the N.Y. Phil, because my first record is N.Y. Phil.

At the Young
People's Concert

CBS Television

"'I have now 4 records of N.Y. Phil, in it 3 record is late Mitropoulos conducted, one is your conducted. [The record Lenny had çonducted was Nikolai Rimski-Korsakov's *Scheherazade;* of the fourth record in his list, a Mitropoulos-conducted Shostakovitch *Fifth Symphony,* Yoshikazu noted: "My first record bought on 2 April 1958."]

"Well, I'm collecting the Great Musicians photo & signature.

"I'm sorry trouble you, would you please send me a your photo to me?

"I entreat this favor of you.

"If possible, please communicate the said to the other members of your New York Phil. Orchestra such as concertmaster John Conigliano; oboe, Harold Gomberg; bassoon, B. Garfield; flutist, John Wummer, and other men of top position.

"I entreat this favor of you.

"I look forward to the day very soon when it will be possible for you to come to Japan."

[*168*]

Lenny and the Philharmonic did go to Japan in 1961.

Teachers frequently write Lenny, often sending along with their covering letters a batch of individual letters from their students. Such a letter came from sixth-grade teacher Richard R. Blackley of the Mark Twain School in Long Beach, California, who wrote:

"The enclosed letters are being forwarded to you at the request of the students involved.

"As a means of enriching my sixth-graders' music program, I taped and shared with them your first Young People's Concert aired in January. We discussed the concert and eagerly looked forward to the birthday celebration for Aaron Copland aired this month. The resultant discussion led to the inspiration to share with you our appreciation for your efforts. We have shared your story of your rise and struggle to your current position and fame, and I honestly add that my pupils and I have a deep appreciation of your courage and dedication to your chosen work. Please be assured that I had little to do with the framing of these letters and that they come from the heart and the sincere desire of each child to communicate with you in a personal way. . . .

"Some of the class insisted on mailing their letters to you separately, feeling that this was more grown-up."

[*169*]

Brother Urban Whitman of St. Joseph Seminary, Teutopolis, Illinois. wrote:

"Just this afternoon I watched your program on Jazz in Serious Music and was very much impressed. Just to tell you of one effect your programs are having—we here at the seminary have a few who dislike serious music and prefer modern or popular music. Interest has been definitely shown now through your interesting and clear explanations to the point that a few of the former dislikers of good music are up for your programs each time and this week more were there than ever. I almost wish your program were a weekly thing. There is so little good music on Television and your manner of bringing good music to the average man can and is doing much to further appreciation of music of all kinds.

"Thank you and may God bless you, your family and your work."

James Wiltz, a grade school music instructor at Metamora (Illinois) Community Consolidated Grade School District No. 1, wrote:

"The children really appreciate you. As a polio victim phrased it, 'Mike, you should watch the program, for Mr. Bernstein is not a 'square' but a 'real cool guy.' I could not begin to have the results if you were not the individual you are to my students."

*At the Young
People's Concert*

CBS Television

Some people write in more or less official capacities, as did Hans Kruger, who wrote,

"As AMERICANISM chairman of Post #33, THE AMERICAN LEGION, St. James, Minnesota and as a GOOD music lover I want to express our most sincere APPRECIATION for the excellent work you do every Saturday afternoon to direct young minds and tastes towards the really GOOD things in life, your program always most INSPIRING and your good humor together with attempts at PERFECTION of good music performance both ENTERTAIN and give ENCOURAGEMENT to those of us who try to improve our future citizens."

Lenny's broadcasts seem to have had some effect, even on the "I Hate Music" kind of audience that Lenny addressed in his song cycle, as a letter from Mary Leslie Turner of Harlingen, Texas, attests:

[*171*]

"In all of my eighteen years, I have never written a fan letter, but I feel that I must show my appreciation for everything that you are doing for we ordinary, everyday people of America. With your television programs, you have opened up a whole new world for anyone who loves any kind of music.

"For years I've loved 'exact' music. I found it by myself, and I've listened to it by myself, for no one seemed to share my interest. I did not know why I love it, but I couldn't help myself. Down here at the 'jumping-off place of the United States,' thirty miles north of Brownsville, Texas, 'exact' music has been practically a dirty word. The vogue around here has been for music like 'Houndawg,' and 'Oh, My Sombrero.' I like this type of music too, you understand. After all, I'm no 'square.' But I have learned not to mention my taste for your kind of music, because people have looked at me as if I had two heads.

"But when your television programs were broadcast on the air, things started changing. People my age stay home on Saturday morning to watch your program, and then they discuss it at school. It is no longer 'square' to love 'exact' music, but sort of a tribute to one's taste. Of course, this changing is slow, and there are still a lot of sceptics, but the difference is there, and it is growing.

"The thing is, you make 'exact' music fun. You make it understandable and enjoyable to even a child. You educate while you entertain.

[*172*]

"Like I said, I haven't known why I like this music, but by watching your programs, I'm beginning to see why.

"Even my father, a real 'he-man' sort of a person who scoffs at lovely music, has been having less and less to say about it. One Saturday morning, he sat down with my sister and I to watch your program. He listened without saying one derisive word, and this is unusual, and he stayed until the program was finished. I could tell that he enjoyed it; he even grudgingly admitted it!

"So you, see your programs are going places. If they are reaching people's ideas down here, Heaven knows what a riot they must be causing in the 'civilized' world further north!

"I don't want you to ever stop your programs. There is so much to learn about 'exact' music, and I don't know of a better way to learn than watching your show. I also have another reason for wanting you to stay on television. When I get married, I want my children to be taught the beautiful world of music by you.

"P.S. Guess what program follows yours? 'Duffy's Tavern'! Isn't that hilarious?"

Not only reluctant fathers but others are moved by Lenny. David Bernard Hill, a Radio Corporation of America engineer, wrote:

"Yesterday, I was alone in my house, (my wife having gone to visit our son in the foothills of Bucks Co.,

At the Young People's Concert

Penn.) I was read out, so I turned on the television, you were there, you were speaking, at first I paid you not much attention, but, dammit man you grew on me, until you had, with that marvelous way you have of explaining music to the laymen, me hypnotized. I have a sister who under the name of Mlle Marie Rossi sang in concert years ago, and had she continued would have reached the heights and it has been her contention for thirty years that I have had a very marvelous tenor voice. I have never used this voice publicly, but I sing for the sheer joy of it, but enough of me (I am 63) and more of you. To my mind you bring more joy to more people with or without understanding of the mechanics of your profession than any one I have had the good fortune to meet up with.

"Some time when the wife and I are in your town may we not have the pleasure of meeting you? She also loves and listens to not only your beautiful music, but being a good piano player can appreciate you and the

[174]

work you do to its fullest extent. Years of good luck to you."

Lenny gets a good deal of mail from aspiring future musicians, such as that from Ronald R. Biscaro, whose story echoes some of Lenny's early difficulties.

"I am a very fond admirer of your conducting and am also a great lover of music. I don't want you to get the wrong impression of me because I would very much like your help. I have been told by many people that you take great pride in helping young students in the music field. This is the field in which I wish to make a career.

"I want to specialize in professional conducting not just because I have seen you on T.V. but because I have always had the inspiration to conduct an orchestra such as the one you have at your disposal. From the time I was 5 years old I have wanted to be a conductor. There was one obstacle to this wish of mine. That was my parents. They said that musicians starve to death. I finally convinced them that I was bound determined to be a conductor or starve because no one can be something that someone else wants them to be.

"I wasn't able to convince my parents until this year and I am already a Junior in high school. I have Participated in Senior Band, Chorus and Orchestra for a total of three years and play an accordion besides playing French Horn.

[175]

"I would appreciate your help and advice on how to go about securing a position in a Professional school of Music, for conducting. [Lenny suggested that he write the Eastman and Julliard music schools for their catalogs.]

"I am taking a regular college entrance course but my marks this year aren't too good because I can't do 11th year math or science with a bad aptitude as the guidance director told me so next year I will get all the music I can."

Ruth Elaine Cardone of Ambridge, Pennsylvania, wrote:

"I was hesitant upon the way I should begin this letter. So I'll begin with a music angle.

"I am 15 years old, and attend Mount Gallitzin Academy in Baden, Pennsylvania. I have been taking piano lessons for the past 8 years, and have played the organ for $3\frac{1}{2}$ years. I also play the trumpet in our School Orchestra. Besides that I am now studying Gregorian Chant. I love music and want to advance myself as much as possible. I am mainly interested in Classical Music.

"I have never as yet failed to see any of your television broadcasts. Your music is so inviting and has so much beauty that I could sit and do nothing but listen to it. In watching you conduct the Philharmonic Symphony on television, I particularly admire the way you go

[176]

with the music and put yourself into it, as though there was nothing else around."

Lenny has also inspired some latterday music students. E. L. Erickson, founder and owner of E. L. Erickson Products in Brookings, South Dakota, wrote:

"I am not a musician but have a considerable appetite (not aptitude) for fine music. Several years back (1945) I began taking piano lessons with my nine year old daughter, starting from 'middle C.' It has not been possible to keep up as I would like but your presentation yesterday has 'fired me up.' "

One letter writer, Edith Corbin of Great Neck, Long Island, New York, might have told her story to Lenny if she had not respected his "night off."

"I literally had to bribe my 12 year old, rock and roll loving, son to tune in on your concert last Saturday. He agreed to give you ten minutes, but ended up savoring every minute of the full hour.

"In that hour you not only 'reached' him, but you gained his respect and admiration. More than that, you opened his mind to another kind of music.

"We spent the rest of the afternoon talking about you, and all kinds of music.

"That evening, while driving into the city, I gave my husband a detailed account of your concert and lecture, and the impression you made on our boy. Together we were grateful to you.

"Imagine, then, how I almost jumped out of my seat, when I found myself sitting across the aisle from you and your charming wife, at the performance of *Look Back in Anger*.

"I must confess, I was terribly tempted to speak to you, but a deep respect for your right to privacy on such occasions held me back.

"My son, when he heard, was very disappointed. He wanted you to know how good your concert was— and how you captured him—and he would have liked to have your autograph!

"We thought you'd enjoy hearing about this small conquest—and perhaps after all, our son Bob might get your autograph. Could you send it?" He did.

Lenny has inspired some of his listeners to write more than letters, as Amy Solit of Brooklyn and Mrs. E. Vigneron of Leavenworth, Kansas, testify. Miss Solit addressed her letter

"Dear Mr. Bernstein and the entire New York Philharmonic,

"Your two shows so far have been the most marvelous Television programs I have ever seen.

"I'm a High School senior and was so deeply moved, by your first show, that when we were asked to write a composition during the State Scholarship Examination,

I picked you as the person who has contributed the most towards our present day society. I explained how much you are contributing towards the growth and development of the children.

"It's a pleasure to watch your shows."

Mrs. Vigneron wrote:

My daughter typed the enclosed letter 5 days ago and told me it was too messy and she wasn't going to send it.

"After reading it I decided to mail it to you, anyhow, misspelled words and all.

"Her term paper is due in a couple of weeks and she is so involved I'm sure she'd never get around to retyping, it (the letter).

"I do hope you enjoy reading it. This is the first fan letter she has ever written."

Linda Kay Vigneron's letter began:

"Thank you so much for being such a fascinating person. Because if you weren't, I would be in a pickle.

"Sir, I have selected you as my subject for my Senior English Term paper and I am quite satisfied with my choice.

"The study of success is always pleasing. It's true that I could have picked any one of a number of people considered by the public to be successful, but to me, 'famousity' is not success in its entirety. Happiness and satisfaction must be included."

Listeners—and letter writers—see likenesses to a great many people in Lenny. Mrs. Lynne Ianniello of Rockville Centre, New York, describes her first exposure to the Young People's Concerts,

"When a six year old monster comes tearing into the kitchen to report 'There's beautiful music on TV,' you go listen too, fast. When that same six year old sits still for a full 60 minutes, you feel his head and if it isn't hot, you decide to write to the person responsible for that hour of relaxation. I enjoyed the program as much as he did."

Then she goes on to make the comparison.

"I don't know whether you will consider this flattery or not, but your facial expressions while talking to the children reminded me of Danny Kaye's in the UNICEF [United Nations International Children's Emergency Fund] films he made. You both looked as though you enjoyed children as people. While he entertained them with laughter you entertained them with music. They can certainly use both."

John W. Keenan of Freeport, Long Island, New York, made an even more startling comparison.

[180]

"I can think of only one other man on television who can hold an audience so completely, by talking and explaining, as you can. That is Bishop Sheen."

He concluded:

"At the risk of sounding like a teen-age fan club member (actually I'm 32, have a wife and two daughters, and work in Research & Development in a chemical plant) I make one more request. I would appreciate your sending an authographed photograph. It would have a place of honor in our 'Music Corner.'"

There is a saying that "a prophet hath no honor in his own country," but Lenny has fans even in the Boston area. Mrs. M. Stanley Livingston of Belmont, Massachusetts, near Boston, wrote:

"I am proud to say that I also come from the area where The Bernstein originated and received his education, and I am sure you are one of the brightest star among the Harvard Alumni.

"You make our house a shambles when your programs occur, because everything must be done before you come on. Lunch is ready ahead of time, and anyone who dares interrupt me on Saturdays when you talk to the children (I put myself in their bracket on these particular Saturdays), can darned well get their own lunch! When you come on on Sundays, if no one wants an early dinner, that's too bad for them!"

She adds, "Inasmuch as my husband is a very down-to-earth longhair too (nuclear physics), and in his field has much the same effect as you in yours, although I can understand yours better, I feel very strongly about inspiring teaching."

Possibly no letter writer's enthusiasm has ever surpassed that of William Boyer of New York City, who wrote:

"If I were President of the U.S. I'd be strongly tempted to make the likes of you a Secretary of State— for more good will comes from the sort of performance which seems innate with you than from the performances in all these diplomatic conferences. After all, Music is a 'Common Language' and you've mastered it!!!!"

Madeline Marsicano of Woodhaven, New York, recorded her whole switch from rock 'n roll to "serious" music:

"I am fifteen years old and to my parents and friends my musical interests have suddenly changed. . . .

"But I think you know that I just didn't mistakeingly turn on the Philharmonic hour one Saturday and say, 'O, this is for me!'

"No indeed; it took time. And it all started with your first Young People's Concert one and a half years

[*182*]

ago. At the time this made very little impression on me, but because of this your succeeding two 'Young' Concerts and an Omnibus show I was prepared for the 'great' change.

"When your first Sunday show opened with Beethoven's 9th on November 30, 1958 the turning point occurred. From then on it has been a joy for me to turn on the radio and listen to my 'newfound' music.

"Handel instead of Presly now blasts from my radio, and I'm glad.

"Finally now, as an end to my eventful year this Sunday, April 5, I have tickets for Carnegie Hall to see the Philharmonic in person.

"I sincerely hope I haven't taken up too much of your time or, oh horrors, bored you, for it was you who 'showed me the light'; the light of beautiful music.

"Thanks!"

Mrs. Ann E. Gearhart of Kalamazoo, Michigan, summarized a broadcast season as follows:

"In your final children's concert of this season you expressed concern as to what, if anything, you have accomplished in this series. I wish, as one chronologically excluded from childhood but still happily able to learn from having been a child, to tell you of the subtle impact your concerts have had on my learning.

"I use the term 'subtle impact' intentionally. Your use of words has sharpened my own understanding of them. The concern and respect with which you forcefully share your knowledge with your audience was appreciated, I'm sure, as much by their youth as by my adulthood. By showing your delight in what you do, your complete respect for the entire field of music and your confidence as a man who is still learning while he is teaching, you command your audience away from musical prejudice toward musical preference and judgment. Your cheerful interweaving of profundity with humor offers something concrete in return for something shadowy; something real from each member of the audience you captivate which chases away capriciously the cobwebs of misunderstanding and fear of greatness. You offer, through yourself and the Philharmonic, not only a glimpse of greatness from without, but a beginning of respect and love of learning from within.

"Please accept my most sincere thanks for creating a great and individual something through your concerts this year, and be assured that you will be joyfully received by a most ready audience next year."

One of my favorite letters—and one that I hope I have in some part here answered as well as Lenny's having answered it—reads as follows:

"I am a ten year old girl very interested in music. I read a lot of books about music, but I would like someone or you to wright a book about you and your whole live up to now.

"I would like to know if you are married or have children.

"If you send me an answer to my letter send it to.
                Carol Jean Bentley
                4033 Tyler
                Berkley, Mich.

"I watch your concerts any chace I get. I think they are very good. They help children as well as adults in music."

I have tried in telling this story of Lenny to show what kind of boy he was, what influences and atmospheres blended to shape his future as a man, and to give some idea of his feelings about music, both in general and in relation to himself.

Lenny is now in his mid-40's; since he was 41, he has been the permanent conductor of the New York Philharmonic. That very fact, that an American-born, American-trained young man should reach that high place in our musical world, has significance surely in terms of our national cultural pride. But most especially, it indicates that our generation, and those that come after, may find their cultural place more easily, whether as active contributors to it, or as well prepared receivers of it.

There is much talk these days, both here and abroad, about the "cultural explosion" in America. Jokes are made about the sudden rash of cultural centers springing up across the country, about our drugstores where

[185]

culture can be bought from racks of paperbacks, ranging in subject from Art to Zen, and of longplay records from Acuff to Szigeti.

The jokes are easy to make; but underneath the excesses and the exaggerations, the truth is, I believe, pretty marvelous. Americans in great numbers have begun to realize what deep pleasure and satisfaction can be made their own by increasingly extensive listening, looking, and reading. Americans are becoming aware of the "sweetness and light"that comes from "acquainting ourselves with the best that has been known and said in the world, and thus with the history of the human spirit," as the English critic Matthew Arnold put it nearly a hundred years ago.

In his way, Lenny has already made a sizable and meaningful contribution to this relatively new American hunger. His continuing efforts as a conductor, teacher, and composer, combined with his extraordinary ability to communicate the inner spirit of music to listeners, should in the years to come help make come true for Lenny one of his most cherished goals—to use everything he knows to encourage the ever increasing exposure to, acceptance of, and joy in music.

A List of Bernstein Compositions

1941-1942

Sonata for Clarinet and Piano. First performance: David Glazer, clarinet, and the composer at the piano, Boston, April, 1942.

1942

Symphony No. 1 (Jeremiah). First performance: Pittsburgh Symphony Orchestra, the composer conducting and Jenny Tourel, mezzo-soprano, singing in the "Lamentations" movement, Pittsburgh, January 28, 1944.

1942-1943

Seven Anniversaries [for piano]. 1. Aaron Copland, 2. Shirley Bernstein, 3. Serge Koussevitsky, 4. William Schuman [the composer, a friend of the composer's since his Harvard days], 5. Paul Bowles [the composer, another old friend], 6. Nathalie Koussevitsky [the maestro's wife], 7. Alfred Eisner [a Harvard classmate who died shortly thereafter of cancer]. First performance: Gordon Manley, Town Hall, New York, October 13, 1944.

1943

I Hate Music: Song Cycle of Five Kid Songs. 1. My Mother Says that Babies Come in Bottles, 2. Jupiter Has Seven Moons,

3. I Hate Music, 4. A Big Indian and a Little Indian, 5. I
Just Found Out Today. First performance: Jennie Tourel,
Town Hall, New York, November 13, 1943 [considered the
first performance though she had sung the song cycle at a
Red Cross benefit in Lenox, Massachusetts, on August 24,
1943.]

1944

Fancy Free, ballet score. First performance: with the Ballet
Theatre's John Kriza, Harold Lang, and Jerome Robbins
[the choreographer] as the three Sailors; Muriel Bentley,
Janet Reed, and Shirley Eckl as the three Passersby, the
composer conducting, at the Metropolitan Opera House,
April 18, 1944.
On the Town, musical comedy score. Book and lyrics by Adolph
Green and Betty Comden, based on an idea by Jerome
Robbins, who staged the musical numbers and choreography,
directed by George Abbott, with Sono Osato, Nancy Walker,
Betty Comden, Adolph Green, Chris Alexander, and John
Battles in the cast. First performance: Adelphi Theatre, New
York, December 28, 1944.

1945

Hashkivenu [a part of the Sabbath service] for mixed voices,
cantor, and organ. First performance: Park Avenue Synagogue, New York, May 11, 1945.

1946

Facsimile, ballet score. First performance: with the Ballet

[*189*]

Theatre's Nora Kaye, Jerome Robbins [choreographer], and John Kriza dancing and the composer conducting at the Broadway Theatre, October 24, 1946.

1947

La Bonne Cuisine, song cycle. [The title is that of a French cookbook, and specific recipes are set to music.] 1. Plum Pudding, 2. *Queues de boeuf* [Oxtails], 3. Tavouk Gueunksis [a Turkish boiled chicken dish], 4. *Civet à toute vitesse* [Rabbit at top speed]. First performance: Marion Bell, soprano, in her New York debut at Town Hall, October 10, 1948.

1947-1948

Five Pieces for Brass Instruments. [Commissioned by the Juilliard School of Music]. 1. Elegy for Mippy [horn and piano], 2. Elegy for Mippy II [solo trombone], 3. Fanfare for Bima [trumpet, horn, trombone, tuba], 4. Rondo for Lifey [trumpet and piano], 5. Waltz for Mippy III [tuba and piano]. First performance: New York Philharmonic Benefit concert, the composer conducting, at Carnegie Hall, New York, April 8, 1959.

Four Anniversaries [for piano]. 1. Felicia Montealegre, 2. Johnny Mehegan [jazz musician and teacher at the Juilliard School of Music], 3. David Diamond [the composer, an old friend], 4. Helen Coates. First performance: Eunice Podis at Town Hall, New York, October 18, 1948.

1949

Symphony No. 2 (The Age of Anxiety), for piano and orchestra. First performance: Boston Symphony Orchestra at Carnegie

[*190*]

Hall, New York, Serge Koussevitsky conducting, the composer at the piano, April 8, 1949. (This music scored for ballet was first performed as a ballet with the same title by the New York City Ballet at the City Center, New York, with Tanaquil LeClercq, Francisco Moncion, Todd Bolender, and Jerome Robbins [choreographer] dancing the principle roles, on February 26, 1950.

1950

Incidental music for a production of Sir James Barrie's *Peter Pan*. First performance at the Imperial Theatre, New York, with Jean Arthur and Boris Karloff in the leading roles, April 24, 1950.

1952

Trouble in Tahiti, one-act opera. First performance: Festival of the Creative Arts, Brandeis University, Waltham, Massachusetts, with the composer conducting and a cast including Nell Tangeman, David Atkinson, Constance Brigham, Robert Kole, and Claude Heater, June 12, 1952.

Wonderful Town, musical comedy score. Libretto by Joseph Field and Jerome Chodorov, based on their play *My Sister Eileen,* derived from *New Yorker* stories by Ruth McKenney, directed by George Abbott. First performance: at the Winter Garden, New York, with Rosalind Russell, Edie Adams, and George Gaynes in leading roles, February 25, 1953.

1954

Serenade for Solo Violin, Strings, and Percussion. First perform-

ance: the Teatro La Fenice Orchestra, Venice, with the composer conducting and Isaac Stern, violin, September 12, 1954.
Score for the motion picture *On the Waterfront*, starring Marlon Brando, released July, 1954.

1955

Incidental music for *The Lark*, a play by Jean Anouilh, adapted by Lillian Hellman. First performance: at the Longacre Theatre, New York, with Julie Harris in the leading role, November 17, 1955.

Prelude, Fanfare, and Riffs for Orchestra. First performance: Omnibus, ABC Television program, "What Is Jazz?" with the composer conducting Benny Goodman's band, October 16, 1955.

1956

Candide, musical comedy score. Book by Lillian Hellman, lyrics by Richard Wilbur, John Latouche, Dorothy Parker, directed by Tyrone Guthrie. First performance: at the Martin Beck Theatre, with Robert Rounseville, Barbara Cooke, Max Adrian, and Irra Petina in leading roles, December 1, 1956.

1957

West Side Story, score for musical play. Book by Arthur Laurents, based on a conception of Jerome Robbins, who also directed and choreographed, lyrics by Stephen Sondheim. First performance: at the Winter Garden, New York, with Larry Kert, Carol Lawrence, Chita Rivera, Mickey Calin, and Lee Becker in leading roles, September 26, 1957.